Welcome

to our comprehensive guide to sea rig construction

Whether you are a shore or boat angler, this bookazine contains rigs for all species and all conditions, with easy-to-follow instructions on how to make them.

We cover the history and development of the rigs, so that you can see the thought processes involved and apply them to your own angling, and we show them in action, in fish-packed features that will give you confidence in their effectiveness.

There really is something for everyone here, with rigs that will catch you fish when conditions are against you, and rigs that can give you the winning edge in competitions.

From dabs to tope, you will find the best rigs to target a wealth of species within these pages, where we cover the best components to use and how to put them together.

These rigs have been selected and assembled by expert anglers from all around the country, so wherever you decide to wet a line you can be sure you have the best fish-catching setup possible.

Making your own rigs is satisfying and enjoyable, and there really is nothing better than catching fish on tackle that you have put together yourself. As you become more familiar with the rigs within this bookazine you will be able to apply your own tweaks and adjustments to them to suit your local conditions, and you will always have the basic designs within these pages to fall back on.

These rigs are proven, tried and tested fish catchers that have worked time and time again, and within these pages we explain how and why they will work for you.

Make up these rigs, use them with confidence, and see your catches improve.

Tight lines

Paul Dennis, Editor

Contents

SHORE RIGS

BOAT RIGS

The ULTIMATE GUIDE To Sea Rigs

Published by David Hall Publishing Ltd. The advertisements and editorial content of this publication are the copyright of David Hall Publishing Ltd and may not be quoted, copied or reproduced without prior permission of the publisher.

Copyright © 2015 / Edited by Paul Dennis / Designed by Rebecca Abbott / Sub edited by David Haynes / Reprographics by Derek Mooney

The Sliding Leger
BASS RIG

One of the simplest rigs to tie and also one of the most effective.

History

This rig came into use during the mid to late 1960s and has since become an all-time classic. It's designed to give maximum bite detection when fishing for bigger bass when deliberately holding the rod and feeling for bites.

It works well over mixed to rough, or very rough, ground at short range when fishing big crab baits, but is also a great rig when fishing estuaries at close to medium range – because even the slightest movement at the hook end can be felt on the rod tip.

How It Works

The rig shown is designed for close-range casting using a maximum of 20lb line from the sliding swivel, so that if the lead weight is snagged in boulders or rocks, the line to the lead will break easily when pulled. The main reel line would be 25lb in this case, but no leader is needed because the weights will be 2oz or less and the casting distance is short.

If this rig is to be used for medium-range casting with potential weights of up to 5oz, then the line between the sliding swivel and the weight needs to be 60lb. In this case you would also use a clear leader of 60lb on the end of the main reel line that, over sand, only needs to be 15lb.

Because the sliding swivel is free to slide on the main line or leader, the hooklength and main line are pulling in exactly the same direction, so the slightest pull by a fish on the hook end is transmitted straight through to the rod tip, putting maximum bite detection into your hands.

Some anglers prefer to replace the sliding swivel with a beaded rig swivel, because the plastic bead body spreads the weight and force of the cast over a wider section of the main line or leader, helping to protect it. This also applies when pulling free from a snag. Because the bead body is so efficient at sliding over the line, this also minimises the pressure felt by the bass as it takes the bait before the line comes tight to the rod tip.

You can make this rig even more sensitive by shortening the hook trace to between six and eight inches long. This

Build Sequence

01 Slide a size 6 rolling swivel onto your main line, or leader.

02 Slide on a black 5mm bead.

03 Tie on a size 6 rolling swivel.

04 To the free eye on the sliding swivel, tie on 20 inches of 15lb to 20lb clear-coloured mono. This takes the lead weight, which is tied direct to the main line with no link when rough-ground fishing.

05 To the end of the swivel tie on six to 15 inches of 20lb fluorocarbon.

06 Finish by tying on a size 4/0 Mustad Uptide hook to the snood.

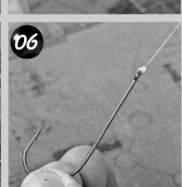

means that as soon as a fish picks up the bait, you will be aware of it. However, in very calm seas, a longer hook trace may be necessary – anything up to 15 inches if the fish are cautious and unsure when feeding in shallow, clear water – and you want the bait further away from the rig swivels and main line, so as not to alert an already spooky fish. This longer hooklength also gives the fish more room to take the bait fully, turn and move away downtide before coming up tight on the rod tip.

It pays when fishing at short range in relatively shallow, clear water to use fluorocarbon hooklengths and line section to the weight as opposed to normal mono. It makes it harder for the eagle-eyed bass to spot the line, which may well be moving slightly in the tide.

If you choose to use a beaded rig swivel instead of the single sliding swivel, and are concerned that the bass may shy away from the coloured bead body, simply colour the red body with a black marker pen to camouflage it.

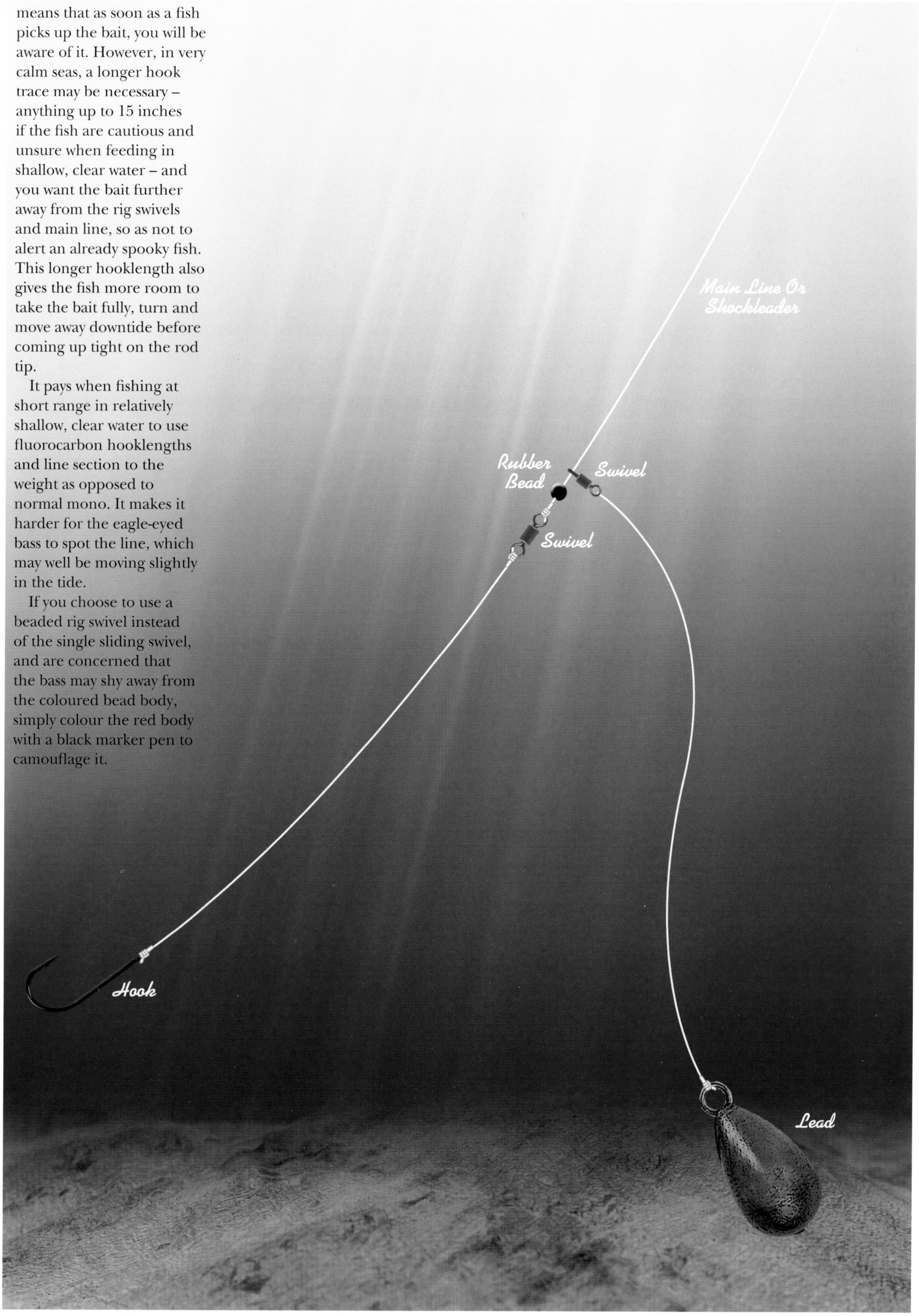

Main Line Or Shockleader

Rubber Bead

Swivel

Swivel

Hook

Lead

Two-Hook Seesaw
WISHBONE RIG

This rig doubles the scent attraction – it's a great flattie rig.

History

Although the 'wishbone' principle of fishing two hooks in close proximity to each other has been evident since the late 19th century, it wasn't until the early 1970s that the modern concept of the wishbone rig came into being. This evolved from the basic one-hook paternoster rig.

There are numerous wishbone designs currently used, but the simple seesaw is a good one to begin with as it is easy to tie, presents baits well, never tangles and is highly effective in all conditions.

For these reasons it's a regular match-winning rig for some of the top rods in the UK. It's also an essential rig for the casual angler, because it scores well with a wide variety of species by fishing two hook baits very close together at medium to long range.

How It Works

The reason the rig positions the Impact Shield within the 2in gap above the lead link is that it gives the Shield room to slide in. This movement means that the hook link won't stretch during a powerful cast. If the Impact Shield had no room to move, the hook link would stretch during casting and the hooks would then not sit tightly in the Shield for future casting.

The advantage of having the two hooks very close together is that the scent trail is stronger and more concentrated. This means that in fast tide runs the scent travels further before weakening. This offers the advantage of pulling fish in towards the baits from much further away.

Equally, in calm seas with little tide run, the stronger

Build Sequence

01 Begin with a 42in length of 60lb rig-body line and tie on a lead link.

02 Slide on a Breakaway Impact Shield, a 5mm bead and a crimp. Fix the crimp in place two inches above the lead link.

03 Slide on a rig crimp, followed by a 3mm rig bead, a size 6 rig swivel, another bead and a crimp. Be sure to leave these loose for now.

04 Tie on a size 4 rig-body connector swivel as the rig-to-leader connector.

05 Take 24 inches of 60lb rig-body line and tie this to the size 6 rig swivel. This heavier, stiffer line will minimise tangles. Tie another size 6 rig swivel to the end of this 60lb line.

06 The hook-link line needs to be 20lb to 25lb, ideally fluorocarbon, but mono is okay, and about 26 inches long. Tie a size 2 Aberdeen hook at one end, slide on a sequin and a rubber rig stop.

07 Pass the free end of the line through the free eye of the swivel tied to the 60lb line, add another rubber rig stop, sequin, and tie on another hook. The rubber stops act as a sliding stop only, allowing the line to seesaw only so far before the rig stop jams up against the eye of the swivel.

08 Finish the rig by putting the hooks in the Impact Shield, then slide the main hook-snood swivel up the rig body until the hook snood comes just tight. Now crimp everything in place.

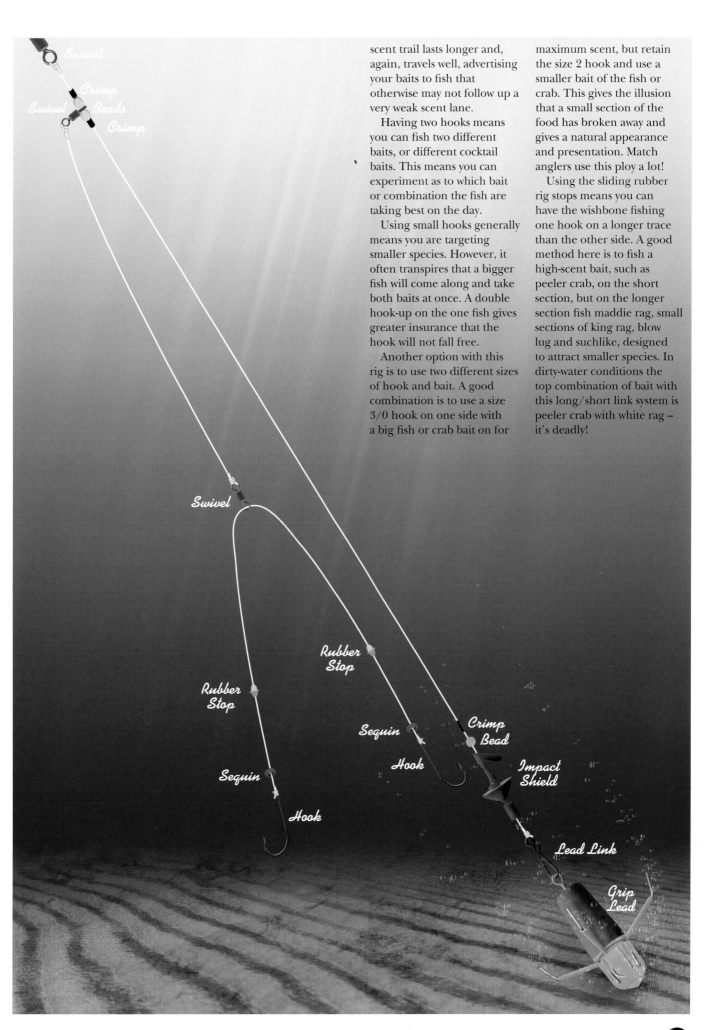

Swivel

Crimp
Swivel Beads
Crimp

Swivel

Rubber
Stop

Rubber
Stop

Sequin

Hook

Sequin

Hook

Crimp
Bead

Impact
Shield

Lead Link

Grip
Lead

scent trail lasts longer and, again, travels well, advertising your baits to fish that otherwise may not follow up a very weak scent lane.

Having two hooks means you can fish two different baits, or different cocktail baits. This means you can experiment as to which bait or combination the fish are taking best on the day.

Using small hooks generally means you are targeting smaller species. However, it often transpires that a bigger fish will come along and take both baits at once. A double hook-up on the one fish gives greater insurance that the hook will not fall free.

Another option with this rig is to use two different sizes of hook and bait. A good combination is to use a size 3/0 hook on one side with a big fish or crab bait on for

maximum scent, but retain the size 2 hook and use a smaller bait of the fish or crab. This gives the illusion that a small section of the food has broken away and gives a natural appearance and presentation. Match anglers use this ploy a lot!

Using the sliding rubber rig stops means you can have the wishbone fishing one hook on a longer trace than the other side. A good method here is to fish a high-scent bait, such as peeler crab, on the short section, but on the longer section fish maddie rag, small sections of king rag, blow lug and suchlike, designed to attract smaller species. In dirty-water conditions the top combination of bait with this long/short link system is peeler crab with white rag – it's deadly!

Improve Your
SOLE FISHING

When the sole are in they're excellent fish to target, because there's no need for long-range casting or complicated rigs. **Roger Mortimore** explains…

There's a longtime myth surrounding the sole, which claims that this delicious flatfish is too wary to catch. It's suggested that the fish is far too bright to take a bait and even if it does take a liking to your offering then its mouth is so small that you won't hook it anyway.

The reality is that the sole is a simple fish to catch – certainly no more of a challenge than any other species – as long as you know how.

The sole, surprisingly, also offers a reasonable scrap because it's all muscle. Quite often, when you've hooked one and it's nearing the beach, it will start kiting all over the place trying to free itself and

give off an electrical signal just as every life form does) or because the bait is held hard on the bottom, but one thing is certain – they work. Sole feed hard on the sea bed and, to ensure the trace is fishing perfectly, you can add a ½oz drilled bullet to the top of your rig.

Top Tip
A ½oz drilled bullet at the top of the rig will keep it hard on the bottom.

Grip leads often work better than plain leads when it comes to hooking-up rates. While a plain lead will drag round in a current and cover plenty of ground, a fish tugging at the bait will also move the lead and may not become hooked. If the rig is anchored firmly with a grip lead, the fish will have more time to swallow the bait and will be hooked instantly as it tries to swim away.

Little Mouths… Big Appetites!

Sole have small, hook-shaped mouths, so the best size hook to use is a size 1 or 2. It doesn't matter whether they're long-shank or short-shank, although if you're planning on releasing the fish then a long-shank version is the way →

Despite their tiny mouths, sole can still swallow quite large hooks, although it does take them a while.

making you wonder if it could be a bass!

And while the sole's name may suggest that it's a loner, it is, in fact, a shoaling fish and when it goes on the feed it can offer terrific non-stop action. It also has the added bonus of being one of the finest fish you could wish to eat.

Booms

While sole can be caught on a variety of rigs, and occasionally take big hooks, ones with wire booms and short snoods seem to give the best results. No-one knows for sure whether this is due to the boom giving off an electrical current (all metals

SOLE FACTS

01 The current British Boat Record for a sole is a fish of 4lb 6oz, caught by M Le Moignan in the Solent in 2006, and the British Shore Record is a massive 6lb 8oz 10dr, caught by Nick Guilmoto on the south coast of Alderney in 1991. However, sole into double figures have been caught commercially.

02 The sole has very small eyes and hunts for food using scent and 'feel'. For this it has a 'beard' of feelers under its chin to locate food, usually worms, but it will also eat small fish, including sandeels.

03 The sole prefers shallow water with a soft, sandy or muddy bottom, as this is where it finds most of its food. Although the sole can be caught during the day, night fishing is generally more productive.

04 The sole will lie buried in sand or mud for most of the day, emerging to feed when tide or conditions suit. When it does feed it is very active, and has been seen standing on its head pushing its mouth into the mud to grab worms.

05 The sole's habitat extends from southern Norway right down to Senegal, including the Mediterranean Sea.

Sole success! This one came out on the first cast.

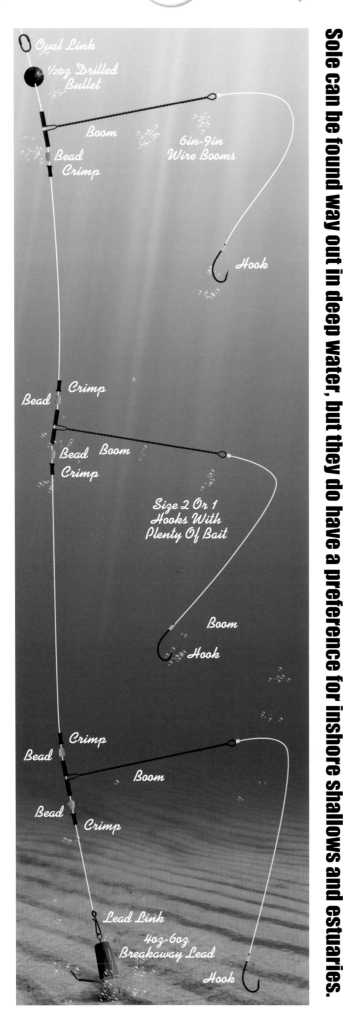

Oval Link

½oz Drilled Bullet

Boom

Bead Crimp

6in-9in Wire Booms

Hook

Bead Crimp

Bead Boom Crimp

Size 2 Or 1 Hooks With Plenty Of Bait

Boom

Hook

Crimp Bead

Boom

Bead Crimp

Lead Link

4oz-6oz Breakaway Lead

Hook

Sole can be found way out in deep water, but they do have a preference for inshore shallows and estuaries.

to go. If a fish swallows the bait on a short-shank hook it will be virtually impossible to retrieve it without damaging the fish, but with long-shank Aberdeens there's every chance that there'll be enough hook showing to extract it without causing the fish any harm.

Despite their tiny mouths, sole are still capable of swallowing quite large hooks of sizes 4/0 and 5/0, although it does take them quite a while. Maybe it's because they're very hungry or that the bigger bait gives off a better scent trail. Whichever the reason, they will slowly ingest bait, probably feeling the hook but unaware of the implications of doing so!

Don't Strike!

Always leave a sole bite to develop into a proper rod-tip pull-over, which usually begins as a series of gentle but steady pulls. On occasions, sole bites can be quite violent, slamming the rod tip over before the line becomes slack, but, even then, leave it! Sole are slow feeders, so give them time to take the bait properly. The worst thing you can do is strike and pull the bait away. Leaving the bite to develop can lead to two things – a well-hooked fish or maybe two or three on the same rig. All flatties are inquisitive, so if one of their 'mates' has found food and is flapping about, others nearby will investigate, resulting in another one of your baits being scoffed.

Casting Distances

Although sole can be found way out at sea in deep water, they do have a preference for inshore shallows and estuaries.

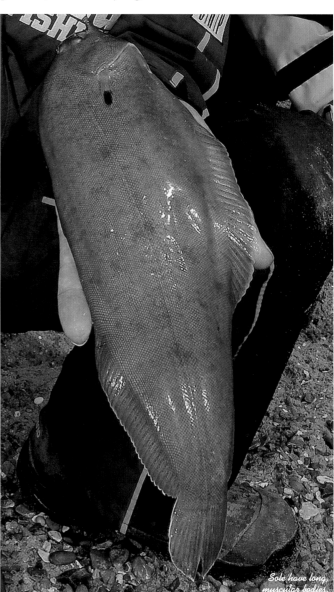

Sole have long, muscular bodies.

This is obviously where their food is, so aim to cast your bait onto worm beds. This often means short casts of 20 to 50 yards. Long casts are only necessary to reach known worm beds that are further out, or during periods of high pressure when fish will move out to the comfort of deeper water.

On occasions, and at some venues, the sole patrol right along the shoreline. At these places you must cast so short that you can see your shockleader knot out of the water. Casting over the fish's heads is usually the main reason for not catching – so always fish with two rods, one close in and the other even closer!

Roger's Revelations...

It was back in the 1960s when I caught my first sole. My brother and I could often be found on a beach somewhere, targeting autumn whiting and codling, and we'd catch the odd sole by accident.

This happened every year and, as I got older, I started to wonder if there were more sole there than we realised. I made some three-hook flappers armed with size 6 hooks – as advised by other anglers – to cope with their tiny mouths.

I did catch a few more by fishing this way, but remembered that we used to get them on size 3/0 and 4/0 hooks piled up with lug or rag. So my thinking changed and I then started to use larger, →

This was one night that Roger got it right – that was some time ago.

The ½oz drilled bullet ensures that the rig lays flat on the sea bed

Sole have beady eyes and small, hooked mouths.

size 1 hooks, which I loaded with plenty of bait. The addition of the wire booms on my rigs, along with the bigger baits, made a huge difference, and my catches went from the odd one here and there to two or three per session.

One memorable trip I recall was when I landed seven sole in the 30 minutes before high water, including three double-shots. The best conditions are usually when it's calm and settled, with high water after dark – there's often a feeding spell at dusk as the light fades on the rising tide.

The most amazing time, though, was during a mid-September gale. I was tucked out of the wind beside a groyne

and landed 10 sole – one at a time. The only way I knew I had a bite was when my line went totally slack and was being blown along the beach instead of pointing into the sea!

That session really was a red-letter day but it came about thanks to a lifetime of learning about these fickle fish. Some of my knowledge has been gleaned from trial and error and other facts learnt by studying the fish's habits and experimenting with rigs and baits – you need to hit all the right notes if you want to be a consistent 'sole man'.

Bait

The most productive baits are harbour rag, king rag, blow lug and black lug. During the summer months, rag tends to produce more fish but, once we get into autumn, lug produces more and bigger sole.

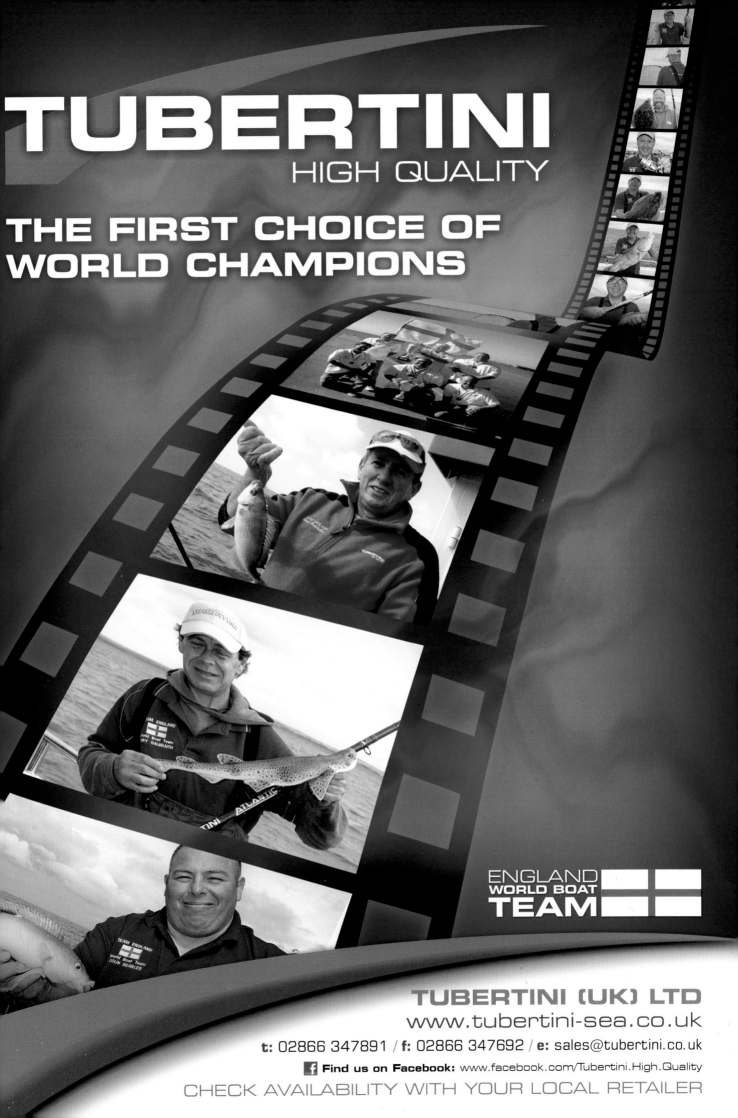

The PULLEY RIG

The go-to rig for rough-ground fishing – especially for bigger species.

History

The pulley rig seems to have originated in both South Wales and the northeast of England around 20 years ago.

The initial pulley principle idea was taken from the standard sliding-leger rig but changed to fish as a normal fixed paternoster rig would. The pulley idea was thought up as anglers in the two named areas were fishing rough ground on a day-to-day basis. They were losing gear and fish when using traditional paternoster rigs due to the trailing lead snagging in the rough ground as the rig or fish was being retrieved.

Although initially designed for rough ground, it also became popular with anglers fishing the shore for rays and tope over clean ground, albeit in a much-modified form.

How It Works

The main advantage of the pulley rig is that when a fish takes the bait, it has the power to pull the hooklength and rig body through the pulley-rig bead and physically lift the lead up out of the snags.

Once the rig body is pulled through the swivel, until it hits the bead above the Impact Shield, the lead is up in the water and above the snags.

The pulley rig works best when casting into a good depth of water. When fishing at range in shallow water the rig lays too flat on the sea bed, and as a fish takes the bait and pulls against the lead, this action can drag a lead deep into a snag.

In deep water, due to the raised angle of the line, the lead tends to literally lift upwards and out of a snag.

Pulley rigs are not a good choice for very shallow-water fishing!

Due to the pulley principle the rig also acts as a self-striking rig. As the fish takes the bait it can pull only minimum line before it comes up tight against the full weight of the rising and sliding lead. It's the weight of the lead that creates the self-striking effect.

Another attribute of the pulley rig is that it can be made to a longer length than other rigs, but remains only half its total length for casting. This means that when the lead reaches the stop bead you have a full length of heavy mono that resists abrasion from fish with rough skin, rocks and barnacles when retrieving big fish over rough ground.

Most anglers choose to build this rig incorrectly by replacing the more expensive pulley-rig bead with a standard-eyed swivel, but powerful casters have found that when using a standard swivel the thin diameter wire of the eye concentrates pressure on the same tiny section of rig body with every cast. This weakens that section of the line and, inevitably, it will part. This occurs during the main power of the cast, resulting in rig-body breakage and the lead weight flying down the beach and causing a potential injury, or fatality, to anybody in the firing line.

The rig described with the Impact Shield is designed when maximum-range casting is required. To save on rig

Build Sequence

01 Start with 50 inches of 80lb rig-body line.

02 To one end of the rig body, tie on a Gemini lead link.

03 Slide on a Breakaway Impact Shield followed by a 3mm bead and crimp. Leave around one-and-a-half millimetres for the Impact Shield to slide, to avoid hook-snood stretch during the cast.

04 Above the crimp, slide on a 5mm bead, a Fox pulley-rig bead and another 5mm bead.

05 Measure the free end of line, leaving it slightly shorter than the main rig body, and tie a double figure-of-eight knot in it to form the hooklength.

06 Tie on either a single size 4/0 Viking pattern hook for rays or, alternatively, us a 3/0 or 4/0 two-hook Pennel rig. When using a single hook, tie in, above the hook, a Powergum sliding stop knot to act as a bait stop when casting.

components when tackle losses will be heavy and distance is less important, do away with the Impact Shield assembly altogether and replace the Gemini lead link with a Gemini bait clip. The hook then just sits in the bait clip, but this rig will not fly as far due to the increased air friction of the bait and not being streamlined by the shield.

When fishing mixed rough ground with heavier 30lb reel line and using a weak-link system to the lead weight, you can also reduce losses by putting a swivel where the figure-of-eight knot should go on the rig body, then adding a hook snood slightly lighter than your main reel line. This will break should the hook get snagged, but remember that a lighter hook snood may also cost you fish.

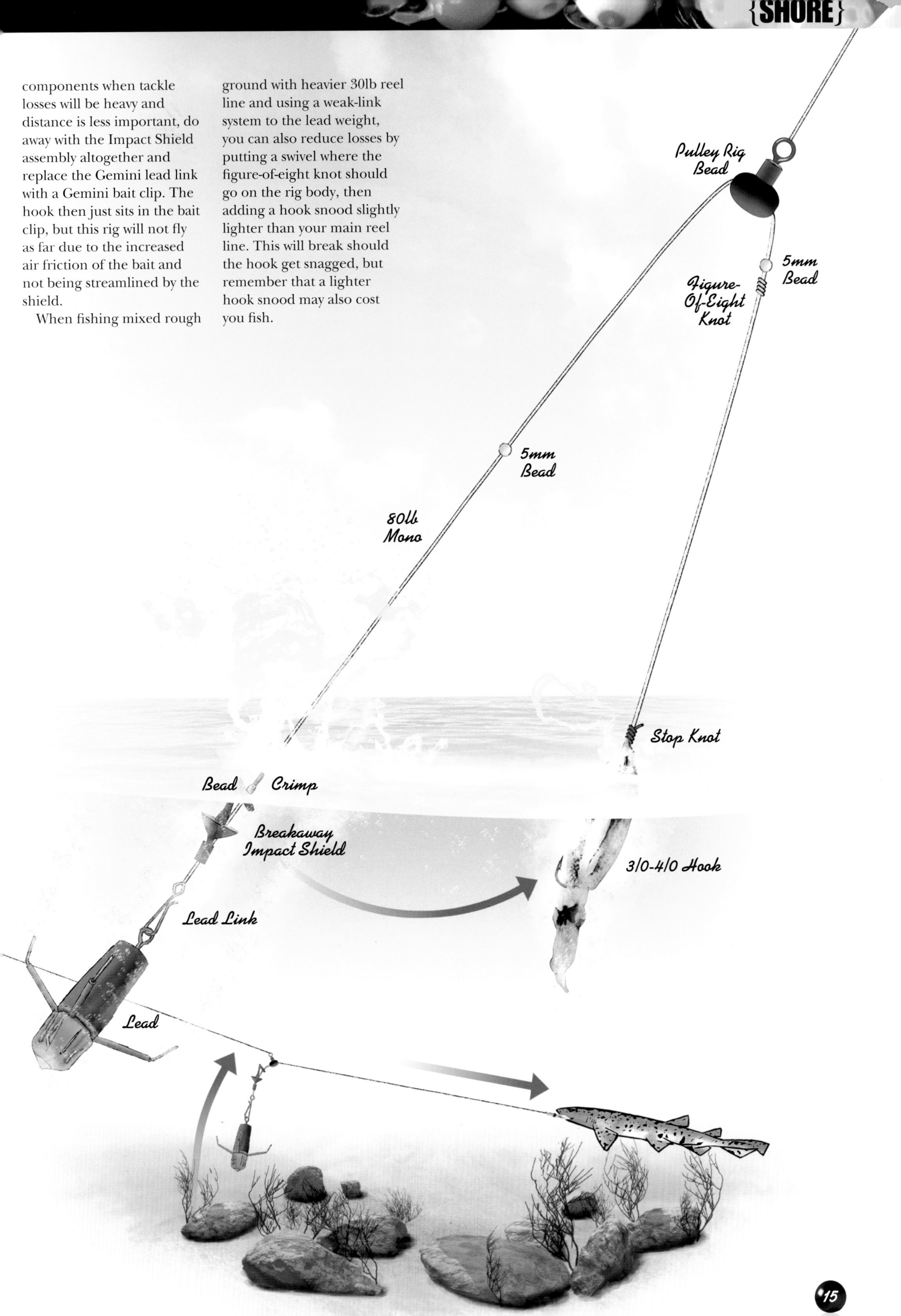

Pulley Rig Bead

5mm Bead

Figure-Of-Eight Knot

5mm Bead

80lb Mono

Stop Knot

Bead / *Crimp*

Breakaway Impact Shield

3/0-4/0 Hook

Lead Link

Lead

Fishing & Beer t-shirt

£16.99 | TEES_001
- Original artwork
- 100% ringspun cotton
- Gildan Premium t-shirts
- Price includes delivery to a UK address

TSF Live To Fish t-shirt

£16.99 | TEES_005
- Original artwork
- 100% ringspun cotton
- Gildan Premium t-shirts
- Price includes delivery to a UK address

Total Sea Fishing logo t-shirt

£16.99 | TEES_002
- Original artwork
- 100% ringspun cotton
- Gildan Premium t-shirts
- Price includes delivery to a UK address

AVAILABLE COLOURS:

 WHITE
 BLACK
 SPORT GREY
 CHARCOAL
 NAVY
 MILITARY
 CHESTNUT
 RED
 ROYAL
 GOLD
 IRISH GREEN
 LIGHT BLUE

LURE

LURE t-shirt

Let the world know what you stand for in your fishing. Proudly displaying the logo of Europe's new LURE magazine.

Size Medium 38" **£16.99** | LURE_002
Size Large 40"   **£16.99** | LURE_003
Size Large 42"   **£16.99** | LURE_004

Price includes delivery to a UK address.

LURE cap

Lure fishing isn't just a sport, it's a culture, and looking good is a huge part of it. A rockin' cap is part of the uniform, and this meshed trucker cap emblazoned with the logo of Europe's new LURE magazine is out there with the best of them.

£10.99 | LURE_001

Price includes delivery to a UK address.

SHOPATDHP.COM
OR CALL
0800 997 8714

 FACEBOOK
Stuff That Anglers Want

 PINTEREST
dhpublishing

 SIGN UP TO OUR E-NEWSLETTER AND RECEIVE SPECIAL PROMOTIONS, NEW PRODUCT LINES AND EVENT REMINDERS. *SEE WEBSITE FOR DETAILS*

ICON

Go Further

FS-SPORT

helping you go the distance

Built on the same design ethos as our M-Sport rods, the new ICON FS-Sport range gives fixed spool users the ability to cast further with no extra effort.

Casting weight – 3.5oz – 6.5oz

Available: 14ft - 15ft - 16ft

Prices starting from £159.99 rrp

One-Up, One-Down
CLIPPED RIG

A great scratching rig for when bites are tough to tempt.

History

This is a rig that is popular with specialist match anglers and experienced freelance anglers. It's an all-year-round rig, but is especially good in the Christmas and early New Year period when bites can be difficult to come by.

It first appeared around the mid 1970s and became popular on the east coast with dab and whiting anglers, as well as on the south coast and along the west coast of Wales for general species, especially plaice. Such is its effectiveness that it is a rig now used nationwide.

How It Works

The main advantage of this rig is that, having the hooks clipped to the rig body, the whole unit flies cleanly, minimising air drag and adding a few yards of extra distance to the cast. The rig can be used for both long-range and short-range fishing.

More importantly, with the baits being clipped in place in the bait clips, it helps maintain excellent bait presentation after the cast by minimising bait damage during the flight. Also, the rubber rig stop and

Build Sequence

01 Begin with 46 inches of 60lb clear mono and, at one end, tie on a Gemini lead link.

02 Slide on a rig crimp, a 3mm bead, a size 10 rolling swivel, another 3mm bead and a crimp. Crimp these in place tight behind the lead link.

03 Slide on a rig crimp, a 3mm bead, a SALT bait clip (inverted) another bead and a crimp. Leave these loose for now.

04 Slide on a rig crimp, a 3mm bead, a SALT bait clip the right way up, another bead and a crimp. Leave these loose for now.

05 Slide on a rig crimp, a 3mm bead, a size 10 rolling swivel, another 3mm bead and a crimp. Again, leave these loose for now.

06 Finish the main rig by tying on a size 4 rolling swivel.

07 Crimp the top crimp, bead and swivel sequence in place just below the top size 4 swivel.

08 To both hook trace swivels tie on 15 inches of 20lb/25lb fluorocarbon, slide on a rubber rig stop and a sequin, and finish with a size 2 Kamasan B940 Aberdeen hook.

09 Put the bottom hook in the bait clip above it, slide the crimp, beads and bait clip up the trace until the hook trace comes just tight, then crimp the bait clip in place lightly; just tight enough so that you can move it under finger pressure.

10 Put the top hook in the bait clip below, slide the crimps and bait clip down the rig body until the hook trace comes just tight, and again lightly crimp in place just so the clip can move under heavy pressure.

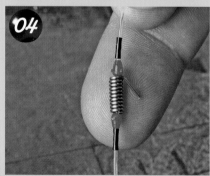

sequin above each hook keeps the bait tight and compact around the hook and again helps preserve good bait presentation, especially when using smaller, more delicate baits.

By only lightly crimping the crimps holding the bait clips in place, it means that under pressure the crimps will slide, avoiding the hook traces stretching under casting load. If the hook traces stretch and elongate after a few casts, the hooks will not sit tightly in the bait clips and will fall free during the cast.

The reason that this rig is so popular is that it has a wide gap between the hook traces. In deeper water, when the line is at a steeper angle, or when fishing the rig at close range, the top hook bait will be bouncing up and down in the tide and surf surge and will take round fish such as school bass, whiting, coalfish, pout and small codling. The lower hook trace fishes hard on the sea bed, being positioned tight behind the lead weight, and is therefore better placed to take more in the way of dabs and flounders, but in summer will pick out plaice, sole and even turbot.

In shallow water this rig fishes well at close range, too, and you can use a slightly slack line between the rod tip and lead to put both hooks on the sea bed to increase catches of flatfish. But, again, by fishing a tight line it will lift the top bait a little and make it behave differently to attract alternative species.

If you're fishing the surf tables, then the fluorocarbon is important because it's stiffer and will tangle less than standard mono. For normal conditions stick with the 20lb to 25lb hooklengths, but in calmer seas and daylight, especially when after plaice, then drop down to 12lb or 15lb fluorocarbon.

A good little trick at night is to add a small 3mm luminous bead between the rubber rig stop and sequin above the hook, and charge this in your headlight prior to casting. This can increase your catch rate when targeting dabs, coalfish, rockling, whiting and codling.

Swivel

Rubber Stop

Sequin

Hook

Bead

Bead

Crimp

Salt Bait Clip

Crimp

Crimp

Beads

Crimp

Swivel

Lead Link

Lead

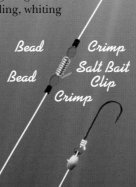

The French CONNECTION

Alastair Gavin strives to acquire the skills of match angling by delving into the Continental style widely used on the south coast of France and other parts of the Mediterranean.

Alastair Gavin and Rachael Jarman show how effective Continental fishing can be.

After entering a large open competition in South Wales and a couple of other events, my knowledge of what match fishing entails has certainly been expanded. But so far I've been relying on a decent fish to make an impact on the rest of the field, when in fact there are other ways of increasing the odds of making your way to the prize table.

While plenty of anglers go for quality in a bid to step onto the match podium, there is a growing band of rods who rely on quantity to regularly scoop up the prizes. It's simply a case of knowing when to go for the tiddlers – and the best method to coax mini species onto the hook.

One of the main things I have learnt during my short match career is to watch other anglers and see what tactics are proving successful. During one of my 'spying trips' I noticed several anglers catching more fish than their rivals by using Continental-style tactics – really long rods and fixed-spool reels. It was this style of fishing that I felt I had to master if I wanted to increase my chances of doing well in a sea fishing contest, and who better to team up with than England international and TSF contributor Rachael Jarman?

The Continental Style

I met Rachael at her house near Minehead, Somerset, and was soon asking her questions about the setup needed for the Continental style of fishing.

She explained: "The Continental style has a lot more finesse than our standard methods, because the target species are so much smaller.

"The rods used are around 15 feet long and have extremely sensitive tips, which will show up the slightest of bite indications.

"Fixed-spool reels complete the combo and they're loaded with ultra-light line and lighter shockleaders than would normally be used along the British coast. Where there are few snags and little tidal flow, the sort of terminal rigs more associated with coarse fishing are employed.

"I fished an event in Italy where my reel line was a mere 4lb coupled with a shockleader of 12lb. Rigs were made up with small hooks – anything from a size 6 downwards – and light snoods with the use of fluorocarbon were common. The rigs themselves can be up to 15 feet long and have pop-ups (small floats on the snoods) incorporated →

21

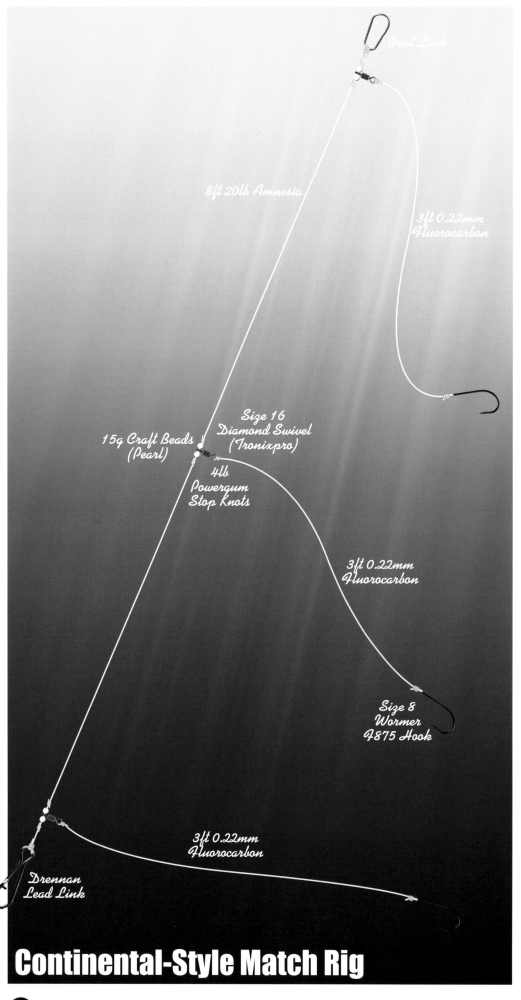

8ft 20lb Amnesia

Oval Link

3ft 0.22mm Fluorocarbon

Size 16 Diamond Swivel (Tronixpro)

15g Craft Beads (Pearl)

4lb Powergum Stop Knots

3ft 0.22mm Fluorocarbon

Size 8 Wormer 9875 Hook

3ft 0.22mm Fluorocarbon

Drennan Lead Link

Continental-Style Match Rig

in them to target fish off the bottom.

"You have to remember that the aim is to catch small to medium-size fish that would certainly not be caught if bigger hooks or stronger line were used. This style of fishing is common throughout the Continent and anyone visiting the shorelines of France, Italy and Spain will see anglers using this gear to devastating effect. Because the water they're fishing in is so clear, the key to catching is all down to light lines and small hooks.

"By using this method, a weight or length of fish can be built, depending on the type of match you're in, and this style of fishing can often prove to be the winning method providing you know when to stick at it and make it work or change to more conventional tactics."

With the theory out of the way, it was time for Rachael – and her husband Wayne – to show me how to put it into practice by taking me to a local mark to them, known as the Blue Anchor.

A First Time For Everything!

This Bristol Channel hotspot, which takes its name from a nearby pub, is at Watchet, Somerset, and is an excellent high-water mark from spring right through summer. But unlike other popular places in the Bristol Channel, Blue Anchor doesn't have particularly strong tidal flows, coloured water or loads of snags, making it an ideal location for our chosen method.

Continental-style fishing is mainly used on clean beaches when the water is clear and, although there was a medium-size tide for our session, this beach is renowned for being virtually snag free.

To simulate match conditions we set up fairly close to each other, and soon had our long three-hook flapper rigs in the water. Having never used a long, sensitive rod in

the sea before – I have always stuck with the standard 13ft powerful beachcasters – I was keen to see what the bites would be like on the 15-footer I had been handed. Rachael's gear was identical, while Wayne went even finer by using a coarse fishing feeder rod. It was clear from the start that this was certainly going to be a session of firsts!

A Matchman Never Stops

While waiting for the first fish to put in an appearance, I took the opportunity to see what Rachael was up to and look at her setup when it comes to match fishing. The first thing I noticed was that she didn't have a box with her to sit on, preferring to stand so that she was ready for the slightest indication.

All her bait and essential tackle items were on trays attached to her rod tripod to ensure that everything was at hand, and no time would be lost fumbling

Although just a small pouting, it could be a match winner.

about in the tackle bag if something needed replacing. Conventional styles mean that you have time to sit down and relax a little, but when you go Continental the aim is to try to reel a fish in EVERY cast.

However, even when bites aren't forthcoming there's no time to relax, because you need to think about changing hook sizes, baits or even rigs in order to induce bites. The difference between winning and losing can be all about

finding the right combination at the correct time.

As Rachael finished her explanation, she pointed to her ultra-sensitive rod tip as it gave a series of sharp taps. She waited for the bite to develop before reeling in the first fish of the session – a small whiting. Although it was a tiny fish, matches can, at times, be won by ounces or centimetres – so fish of any size can play a crucial part in deciding the outcome of a contest. →

Rachael casts her delicate three-hook flapper in search of any fish that might be out there.

Result! This is what Rachael is after – a full house.

Presentation – There's No Excuse...

The way Rachael baited up for her next cast was extremely interesting, for she paid serious attention to detail. By using a baiting needle she was able to put small pieces of rag and blow lug – tipped with a sliver of squid – onto her tiny hooks on the delicate rig for perfect bait presentation. The whiting had fallen for her bottom hook where a sliver of mackerel instead of squid had been placed, so I decided to copy that combination. I spent some time getting the presentation spot on and within seconds of the bait hitting the water there was some visible movement on my rod tip.

All Too Soon

With my rod tip indicating serious interest I couldn't help but strike, totally forgetting the fundamental rule… let the bite develop! The thing about using such fine tips is that everything is magnified, so what may look like a positive indication is merely a fish nibbling at the bait. I certainly didn't

A nice tidy workstation is essential for successful match fishing.

make the same mistake the following cast when the tip started vibrating. Instead of striking I lifted the rod out of the tripod, held it 90 degrees to the sea and felt for another bite before lifting into the fish – a small pouting… and another lesson learnt.

A Frenzy Of Activity

As the tide rose the fish were really on the feed and each cast produced a flurry of activity as fish homed in on the baits. It was now time to

get into a routine – a trick all top match anglers use – and by baiting up, casting, lifting into a fish, rebaiting and casting again a weight or length of fish can soon be built up. Rachael showed exactly how it should be done and was quickly into a rhythm, which had her doubling my catch rate – although as the light started to fade I felt that I was getting into my stride. With the last cast I went all out for the first three-shot of the day, only to find Rachael beating me to it

with her final effort. We had lost count of the number of whiting and pouting we caught, and although I felt I had learnt enough to give this style a go in proper match conditions… something concerned me.

Don't Be Fooled

My worry was that while we had caught a serious amount of small fish, would anglers targeting more sizeable specimens have made our efforts in vain? Rachael was quick to explain: "The key to doing well in matches with the Continental style of fishing is very simple. You need to know when to start on it, when to stick at it and when to switch to more conventional methods, and all this only comes with experience.

"While the baits used with this style may be small, there is always the chance of the unexpected. I remember fishing this mark with ultra-light gear and hooking into a 20lb blonde ray! I managed to play it gingerly right to the shore, and only lost it when it made a final dash and snapped the trace."

Norway: Europe's Best Sea Fishing

Norway Nature Travel

DinTur

20 YEARS AS LOCAL EXPERTS 1996 - 2016

RGF REISEGARANTIFONDET -rgf.no-

Strike your next big fishing adventure and

BOOK NOW for 2016 and 2017

Each year thousands of anglers are coming to fight big fish in Norway – the reasons are clear:

- An abundance of big fish
- Staying in high standard holiday houses
- Self-drive boat fishing
- Shore fishing in the top spots
- Service-minded hosts
- Breathtaking coastline
- Midnight sun and northern lights

**Looking for great offers?
Get up to 50% discount at
www.dintur.no**

Three-Hook
WHITING RIG

This variation on a popular rig is tops for toothy winter whiting.

History

The three-hook rig in numerous forms has been around since the late 19th century, mainly due to its ability to catch a wide range of species in various sea conditions. It is popular with both competition and freelance anglers and is likely to be found in pretty much every experienced angler's rig wallet.

However, the rig we're showing here can be adapted to target specific species better than the standard three-hook rig design can. With the whiting season about to start, the additions we'll make to this rig here will enhance its ability to catch whiting, without unduly affecting its overall catch rate.

How It Works

The crimps being left either side of the bait clips just able to slide under pressure achieves two things. Firstly, when the hook is placed in the bend of the clip for casting, under casting pressure the bait clip can move slightly to the pull of the hook as the rig-body line stretches. The clip being able to move means that the hooklength will not become stretched under casting pressure, which would result in the hook being loose in the clip on future casts without that sliding adjustment.

Secondly, whiting have sharp, needle-like teeth and can scar a hook snood line easily, resulting in weakness and the need to renew the snood. With the bait clip able to slide under pressure, a new hook snood is also easy to replace without the need for exact measuring to position the

Build Sequence

01 Start with 54 inches of 60lb mono and at one end tie on a SALT lead link.

02 Slide on a rig crimp, a 3mm bead, a SALT bait clip, then another 3mm bead and rig crimp.

03 Now slide on a rig crimp, a 3mm rig bead, a size 10 rolling rig swivel, another rig bead and a crimp. Leave these loose for now.

04 Repeat steps 2 and 3 twice more.

05 Complete the rig with a strong size 4 rolling rig-connector swivel.

06 The first hook-trace swivel needs to be crimped one inch below the rig-connector swivel. The middle swivel should be about 18 inches down from the rig-connector swivel, and the third crimped in place 32 inches down from the rig-connector swivel.

The top hook trace needs to be the longest at about 15 inches, with the second hook trace measuring 13 inches and the bottom hook trace being the shortest at just 10 inches. Use 20lb fluorocarbon or clear mono line.

07 Onto each tied hook snood slide a rubber rig stop, a luminous-green bead or beads to form a bait stop, and finish by tying on a Kamasan B940 Aberdeen size 2 or similarly patterned hook.

08 Lastly, place each hook into the bait clip below and slide the bait clip up or down until the hook snood pulls just tight. Leave the crimps either side of the bait clip tight, but still able to just slide on the line under pressure.

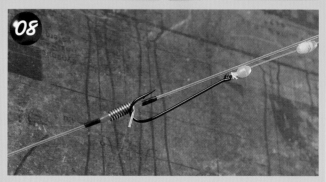

hook correctly under slight pressure inside the bait clip. A simple adjustment of the bait clip, up or down, is all that is necessary.

The reason that this rig features fluorocarbon hooklengths is because fluoro is a harder, more resilient line than mono and will withstand a whiting's teeth better.

All three hooks are placed inside the bait clips for casting, and as the lead weight hits the sea bed the hooks will fall free and flow out in the tide to fish naturally.

The rubber rig stops above the hooks are important. These, and the bead or beads below, act to stop the bait on the hook blowing back up the snood under air pressure during the flight of the cast. This maximises bait

presentation on the hook when it reaches the sea bed.

The different length hook snoods provide slightly different presentation of the bait, with the upper hooks moving more in the tide and slightly up off the sea bed, while the shorter lower snood will be hard on the sea bed. Bigger whiting tend to take a moving bait better than a static one.

The key difference is the addition of the one or two luminous-green beads above the hook. The whiting is one fish that's been proven to be attracted to a luminous-green colour in the water. This simple modification can dramatically increase your catch rate, especially in slightly coloured water and when night fishing.

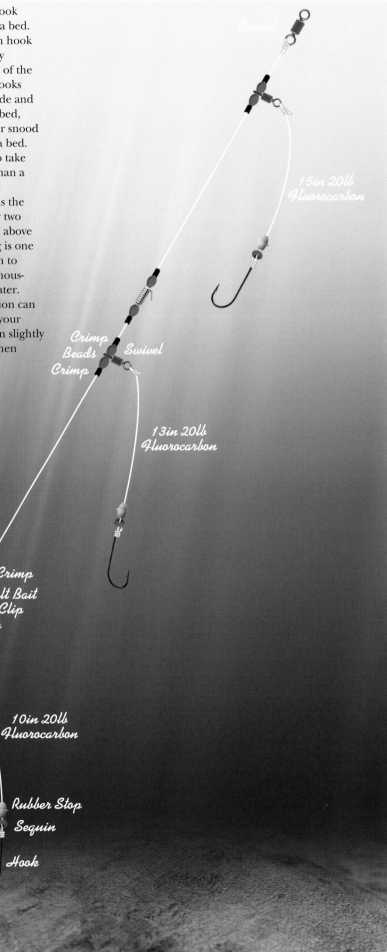

Swivel

15in 20lb
Fluorocarbon

Crimp
Beads
Crimp

Swivel

13in 20lb
Fluorocarbon

Bead   Crimp
Bead   Salt Bait
        Clip
    Crimp

10in 20lb
Fluorocarbon

Rubber Stop

Sequin

Hook

Lead Link

Three-Hook POP-UP RIG

A hook popped up well off bottom targets mid-water feeders.

History

The pop-up rig's history is based way back in the late 1800s. Anglers thought up the idea of adding a small amount of cork behind the bait to lift it off the sea bed. The cork also gave the bait some natural movement and kept it away from scavenging crabs. This was typically used on a long, flowing-trace rig. It needed careful adjustment of the size of the cork used to give the bait just enough lift to get the bait up, but still keep it close to the sea bed for fish to find.

In more modern times, anglers fishing baits over dense sea-bed weed would add cork and, sometimes, small pieces of camouflaged polystyrene behind the bait. This keeps it above the weed to avoid being covered. The method took a lot of congers back in the 1970s from marks in South Wales and the southwest.

Over the last decade or so, those fishing from the shore at Pwllheli in northwest Wales for black bream have developed a rig that uses a sequence of buoyant float beads behind the baits. This method deliberately lifts the bait off the sea bed. Anglers have found the tactic extremely successful – bagging not just bream, but many other species such as dabs, flounders, eels and garfish.

In turn, competition anglers also picked up on to the idea, and they now use pop-up rigs to gain extra species and bites when match fishing.

The advent of the longer rods, which are ideally suited to light-line match fishing, have also seen this rig grow in overall length to target not just sea-bed and bottom feeders, but also to take mid-depth feeders in water up to 12 feet deep.

How It Works

The rig described is designed to fish the two lower hook traces on the sea bed, targeting obvious bottom feeders such as flatfish, whiting, school bass, rockling and dogfish.

The top popper trace, at anything up to 32 inches long, is designed to fish up into mid-water, or in shallow water more toward the sub-surface level. This is especially effective during summer for garfish, but it will also pick off shoaling pout and even the odd mackerel.

The length of the top trace is key to obtaining extra bites from bottom-feeding fish. If you decide to fish the two lower traces as normal with the bait sitting hard on the bottom, you'll find that you pick up extra fish by having the top trace just 12 inches long with the most forward bead three inches away from the

Build Sequence

NOTE The rig described is for use with longer rods, but the same design works well with traditional-length beachcasters; just reduce the overall length of the rig to suit your casting style.

01 Begin with seven feet of 60lb clear mono and at one end tie on a Gemini Lead Link.

02 Slide on a rig crimp, 3mm rig bead, a size 10 swivel, another rig bead and a crimp. Add two more sequences of crimps, beads and swivels above this to give you three hook-trace points in total. Leave these loose for the time being.

03 Complete the rig body by tying on a size 4 rolling swivel.

04 Crimp the first trace swivel in place 12 inches above the lead link. The second trace swivel needs crimping 33 inches above the lead link, with the third trace swivel positioned just below the top connector swivel. The lowest hook trace is 10 inches long, the middle hook trace 14 inches. The top hook trace can be as long as 32 inches if you want to fish up into mid-water.

05 The top hook trace is the popper. Slide on a rubber rig stop, then three or four very buoyant float beads, followed by another rubber rig stop. The rubber rig stops allow the beads to be repositioned on the trace to alter bait movement.

06 Hooks for this rig vary, but they are generally Kamasan B940 Aberdeens in size 6 to 2. These hooks are lightweight, but strong and sharp.

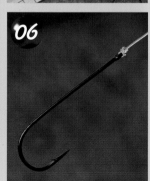

hook. The 3in gap gives the bait freedom to move in the tide and attract inquisitive fish such as plaice, flounders and bream. These species see, then approach, the colour of the beads. The moving bait will lift up off the sea bed for them to intercept.

When fishing in rising weed and kelp, having the bait suspended among the weed stalks works much better than having it sat on the sea bed. Hook traces between eight and 18 inches long work well for codling, coalfish, bream and wrasse.

One of the worst scenarios for anglers is when fishing over stones that are covered in fine soft silkweed. This clogs the line and will, literally, bury baits and minimise scent leaching out making it hard for fish to find. If this is the case change all three hook traces to short 8in lengths and add beads to each hook trace, still leaving a 3in gap between the forward bead and the hook. The bait sits on top of the weed and avoids being smothered and lost to passing fish. This is an exceptional bream rig, but it also scores well with wrasse, including mini species of wrasse such as corkwing and goldsinny.

You also need to think about your hook-trace breaking strains when rigging the hooks. The lighter the hook and line the less buoyancy you need to give the bait movement.

Always experiment with float bead colours. A mix of blue and white works well for the flounders and bream, plaice like yellow beads broken up by red or black, garfish also take baits in front of blue and white or all white, and smaller silver-coloured beads can pick up smaller pouting. Eels also seem to favour silver beads.

Another trick is to vary the gap left between the hook and the beads. That's why this rig is rigged with the beads between sliding float stops or line stop knots – readjustment is quick and simple. Often just increasing the gap by a couple of inches can induce more bites, especially in very clear, shallow seas.

When using very small baits to tempt smaller fish in clear shallow water, it's important to have just enough lift from the bead, or beads. This will, occasionally, allow the tide or gentle surf to lift the bait up off the sea bed and drop it back down, triggering bites when nothing else works.

Size 4 Rolling Swivel

60-80lb Rig Body

34 Inches

32in Snood

21 Inches

14in Snood

Crimp
Beads   Swivel
Crimp

10in Snood

12 Inches

Size 6 To 2 Hook

Rubber Stop

Floating Beads

Rubber Stop

Lead Link

Lead

Three-Boom
SCRATCHING RIG

Enjoy a boom in flattie sport with this tangle-free rig.

History

This is an old rig design having been in use with brass booms from the late 1800s and it was particularly popular between the war years right up to the early 1960s. The brass booms were usually tied in place at a fixed point on the rig.

By the mid-1960s, clear hard-plastic strip booms replaced the brass, then by the mid-1970s plastic-arm-type booms came in that could be rounded at the end with heat to form a junction point and be fixed either inside a three-way swivel with the middle eye removed, or trapped between a closed blood loop knot. In the mid-1980s plastic booms able to rotate on the main rig body line and held in place by stop knots, and eventually crimps, took over and remain the favoured method to this day.

The three-boom scratching rig is a firm favourite with both match and freelance anglers and will often outfish current modern rigs, especially for flatfish, so is a 'must have' in your rig wallet.

How It Works

This rig is particularly effective for teasing out fish during the traditionally quiet February to April period, but is a good all-round general flatfish and smaller species rig throughout the year. It works especially well for flounders, rockling, dabs, plaice, sole, pouting and poor cod.

The rig works well at very close range but you need to know how best to fish it. With the booms being well spaced apart, if you have the line tight between the lead weight and the rod tip, the top hook, and possibly the middle hook, depending on the steepness of the angle of the line, will be up in the water and potentially above the typical feeding zone. It will fish best on a slack line allowing all three baits to sit on the sea bed; you watch the bow in the line for lift takes to identify bites rather than watching the rod tip.

Build Sequence

01 Start the rig with 60 inches of 60lb rig-body line and tie a Gemini lead link to one end.

02 Slide a protective knot sleeve over the knot to the lead link to protect the knot from sand abrasion.

03 Slide on a rubber rig stop, a boom and another rig stop. Add two more separate rig stop and boom combinations to give you three booms on the rig body. Avis booms are a good choice.

04 Complete the rig with another knot protector sleeve and a size 4 rig connector swivel.

05 Slide the rig stops into position on the rig to space the booms apart evenly. A good combination is to place one boom at the top, one in the middle and one about 10 inches above the lead link.

06 You can use short, 9in to 12in, 12lb to 20lb hook snoods as a guide, but shorter 6in snoods can sometimes work well for dabs. Fluorocarbon hook snoods work best in all conditions, but mono is okay. Snood strength can be as little as 6lb for clear-water conditions, but up to 25lb for rougher seas at night.

07 Sequins or beads above the hook can also give you an edge when fishing clear-water conditions. Silver and gold sequins are good choices for daylight fishing, with luminous yellow/green beads being good night-time bankers.

08 Hooks should be Aberdeen patterns in size 2 to 6. Drop down to size 6 if bites are few and far between.

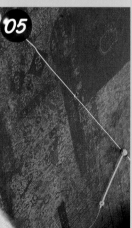

Start with the first boom positioned 10 inches above the lead, the second at about 30 inches, and the third just below the top swivel. Watch carefully for which boom is catching the most fish. If it's the lowest boom, slide it down to just above the lead and slide the top two closer to it. You'll find that two or even all three hooks might start to catch. If only the top hook is catching, slide the lower two up the rig to increase your catch rate.

The booms are not just there as spreaders to keep baits well spaced, they also prove adept at reducing tangles when fishing close in among the surf tables as they keep the hooks well away from the main rig body.

You also decrease the risk of tangles further by using fluorocarbon lines instead of mono. Fluorocarbon lines tend to be a little stiffer than mono and are less likely to wrap around the rig and rarely loop inside themselves to potentially create a weak, unwanted granny knot in the hook trace.

There are occasions when flatties refuse baits presented on plastic booms. This is rarely a visual thing but more of a bait presentation problem. In this case you can use metal booms, which are still available. The extra weight of the metal boom means that with slack line the baits tend to stay tighter to the sea bed, even when passing surf tables pass overhead. With plastic booms a passing surf table can lift the booms up and flatfish in cold winter water may not always be willing to give chase to a lifting bait.

Also think about the boom colour and choose translucent booms for daylight fishing, not darker ones. Some anglers say that red booms attract fish, but others tend not to use red booms by daylight, preferring to match the ground composition. Obviously, black booms would be a good choice over rougher mixed ground.

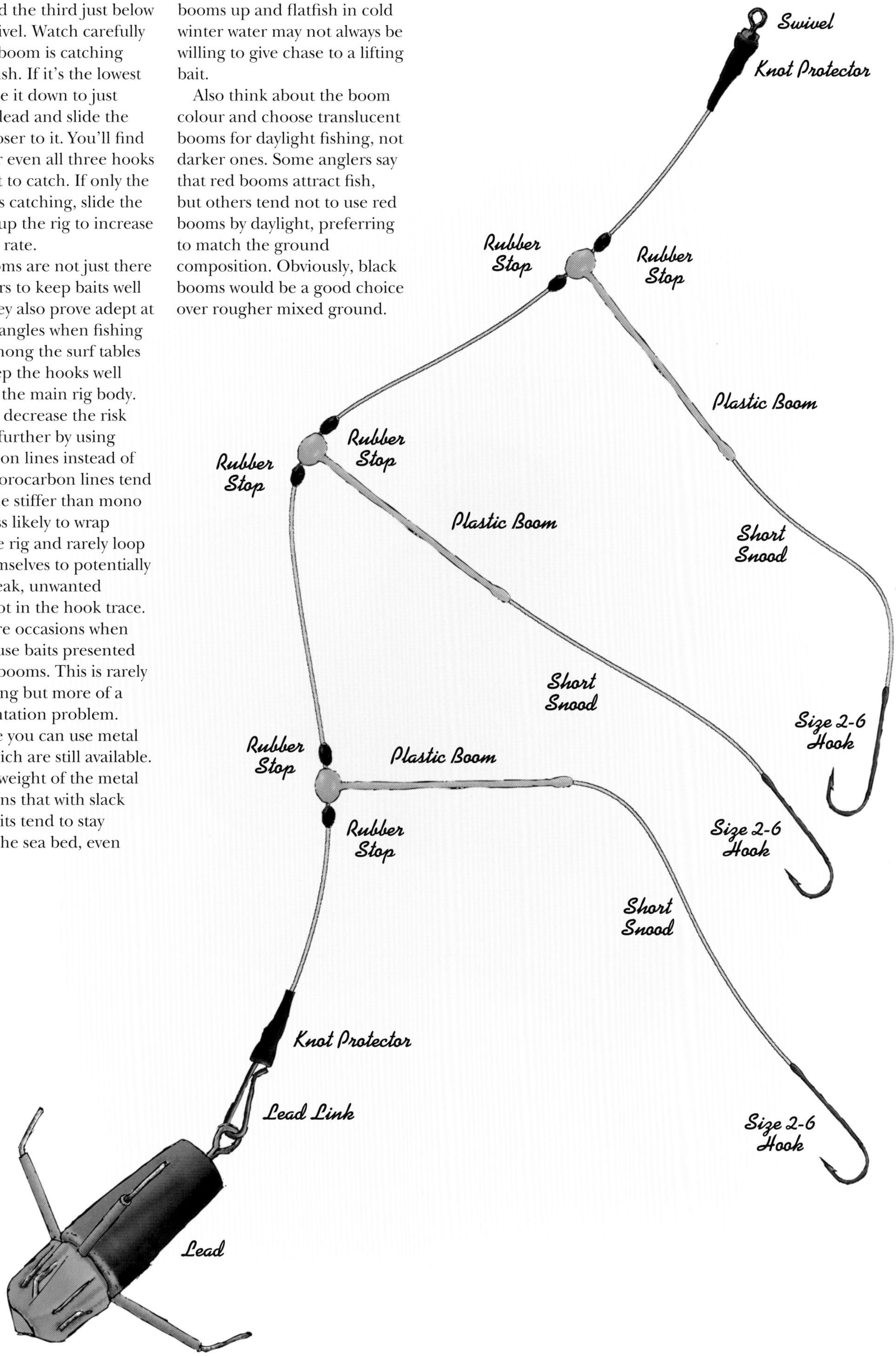

Swivel

Knot Protector

Rubber Stop

Rubber Stop

Plastic Boom

Rubber Stop

Rubber Stop

Plastic Boom

Short Snood

Short Snood

Size 2-6 Hook

Rubber Stop

Plastic Boom

Size 2-6 Hook

Rubber Stop

Short Snood

Knot Protector

Lead Link

Size 2-6 Hook

Lead

Three-Hook Reversible
FLAPPER RIG

The flapper rig covers a number of options and encourages experimentation.

History

This is one of the most successful rigs, and a clone of the first three-hook flappers that became popular for both match and freelance fishing during the early 1970s.

Anglers often quote it as being the ultimate all-round rig, but it's actually the reversible flapper that offers the most versatile fishing. It is a rig that all anglers should have in their rig wallets when targeting general species.

How It Works

So why is the three-hook flapper design so successful? Firstly, it positions three hooks relatively close together, producing a wide and strong scent trail that fish can follow easily to find the baits.

You can use different baits on the different hooks to experiment on the day and see what bait, or bait combination, is most successful. This simple trial-and-error process will make a massive difference to your overall catch rate more often than not.

Secondly, and this is the key to this particular rig, is that the three hooks present baits differently. When fishing to a tight line, the lower hook sits close to or on the sea bed and targets flatfish, the middle one has more movement in the tide and will take a variety of both round fish and flatfish, and the top hook has even more freedom and appeals mostly to round fish hunting just up off the sea bed, such as whiting and coalfish.

Also notice that the lengths of the hook traces vary. A common mistake is to make all the hook traces of an equal short length on three-hook rigs. When you're fishing to a tight line at close to medium range, this kind of rig cannot sit flat on the sea bed. This often results in fish only being caught on the bottom hook trace with the other higher-positioned hooks almost redundant because they are not in the fishes' feeding zone.

The rig described uses a longer top and middle trace; it's designed like this to keep the baits tighter to the sea bed and in the fishes' feeding zone when fishing at close to medium range – without the need to fish a slack line between the rod tip and lead weight. They also encourage more natural movement, which can increase the number of bites you receive.

However, when conditions are calm and you're fishing at close range, by fishing a tight line between the rod tip and lead weight, the top two hooks can be deliberately lifted up off the sea bed a little to lift the baits up periodically, as a surf table passes overhead, away from the sea bed, and target active swimmers such as whiting and coalfish.

Where the 'reversible' bit comes in is that by having a link at both ends of the rig body, you can literally turn this rig around. For instance, if all the fish are coming to the bottom hook, with the lower hook trace positioned well up above the lead, reverse the

Build Sequence

01 Start with about 64 inches of 60lb clear mono, and tie on a SALT lead link at one end.

02 Slide on a rig crimp, a 3mm ovalised rig bead, a size 10 swivel, another rig bead and a crimp. Repeat this sequence to give you three full sets of crimps, beads and swivels. Leave these loose for now.

03 Complete the rig by tying on an inverted SALT lead link.

04 The first hook-trace swivel needs to be placed just one inch below the top

SALT lead link. The middle swivel should be positioned exactly 17 inches below the top swivel, and the third again 17 inches down from the middle hook-trace swivel.

05 The top hook trace needs to be the longest at about 15 inches, the second hook trace should measure 13 inches, and the bottom hook trace will be the shortest at just 10 inches. Each hook trace should be made from 25lb mono or fluorocarbon and finished with a size 2 Kamasan B940 hook for general species.

rig so that what was the top hook now fishes tight behind the lead, with the middle hook now positioned where the first one was before you reversed the rig around. This now puts two hooks in the feeding zone, giving you the chance to double your catches.

This versatility not only increases your catch rate, but also means that you need to carry fewer rigs, although you still have all the options available to you.

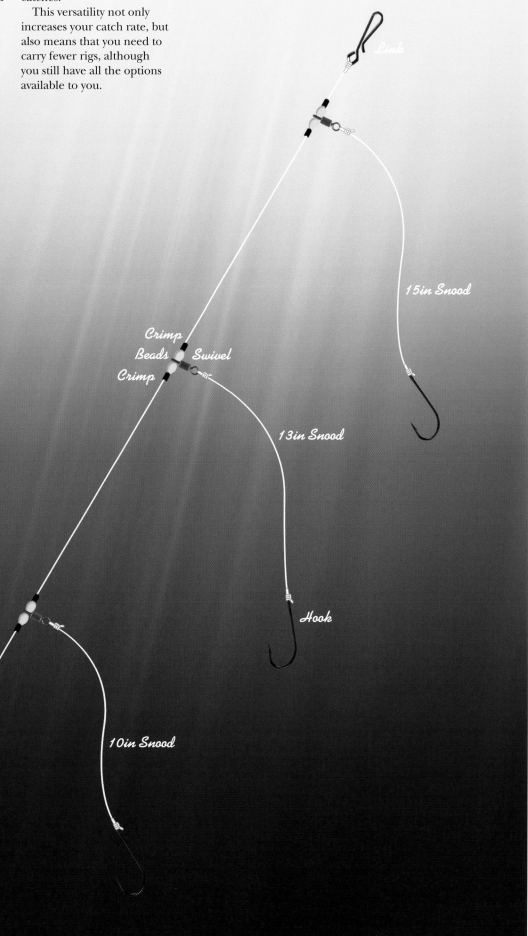

Link

15in Snood

Crimp
Beads   Swivel
Crimp

13in Snood

Hook

10in Snood

Lead Link

ELEVATOR RIG

A long-casting rig that presents a flowing trace when the lead has settled.

History

No-one is really sure about where the concept for this rig originated. Anglers in Wales, Hampshire, East Anglia and on the northeast coast all lay claim to it, although a couple of Scottish shore match anglers were using a rig not too dissimilar to the original quite a few years ago, but they kept it quiet.

It's called the 'elevator rig' because the hook trace moves up and down. When casting, the trace is positioned where a normal clipped-down rig would be, but when being fished it is able to slide down to the lead.

The original rig used a loop of line to hold the Cascade swivel in place, but that has been replaced with an alternative system to suit general fishing much better and reduce the clutter when constructing the rig.

How It Works

When set up, the rig works like a normal clipped-down paternoster and is capable of being cast to maximum range because it's streamlined with the bait directly behind the lead. As the lead hits the water, the line pressure falls slack, the inverted Gemini link flips up and the hook trace releases naturally. As the rig falls through the water column, the water pressure means that the trace remains at the top of the rig. But as the lead hits the sea bed, gravity and tidal pressure mean that the hook trace slides down the rig to fish the bait hard on the sea bed, flowing-trace style.

The rig uses a Sakuma sliding rig crimp above the bait shield so that the hook trace can be replaced should it become damaged during fishing. It also makes it easy to

Build Sequence

01 Take 42 inches of 60lb clear mono. At one end, tie on a Gemini lead link.

02 Slide on a Breakaway Impact Shield followed by a 5mm bead, a Sakuma sliding rig crimp and another 5mm bead.

03 Slide on a Breakaway Cascade swivel via the large eye.

04 Finish the main rig by tying on a strong size 4, three-way rolling swivel.

05 To the middle eye of the three-way swivel, clip on a Gemini lead link, which will sit inverted.

06 The hook trace is 30 inches of 40lb fluorocarbon or clear mono. Finish the hook trace by sliding on a 5mm bead and tie on a Mustad Viking 79515 hook, size 3/0 or 4/0 for rays and cod.

07 Above the hook, tie on a Powergum stop knot to hold the bead in place and act as a bait stop.

08 Place the hook in the bait shield, slide the Breakaway Cascade swivel up the rig body and clip it into the inverted Gemini link. Hold this in position as you slide the bait clip and hook downwards to set the correct tension for casting, so the hook remains set in the shield.

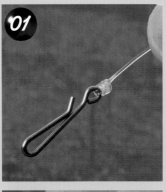

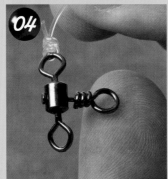

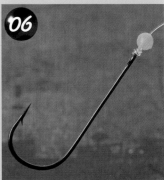
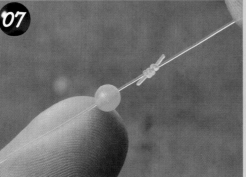
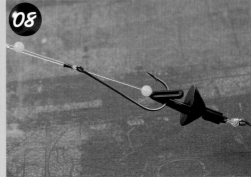

adjust the bait-shield position without being too precise about the new trace length. To prevent the hook trace stretching during powerful casting it's also best to have the bait shield sliding a little.

The use of a quality three-way rolling swivel must be stressed. Do not confuse these with cheaper barrel swivels, which do not have the strength for maximum

power casting. However, rolling swivels do have the strength and can be cast with confidence.

Built as shown, the rig can be used for long-range beach fishing for rays and turbot, and in deeper-water situations at long range for bass, cod and huss.

You can reduce the breaking strain of the hook trace to 20lb and drop the

hook to a size 2 Aberdeen pattern to target flatfish, gurnards and codling off beaches and rock ledges – also piers, jetties and harbour walls when long casts are needed.

This very reliable rig can also be used for uptide fishing off the boat when targeting rays, smoothhounds, bass, cod and big flatfish – with great success.

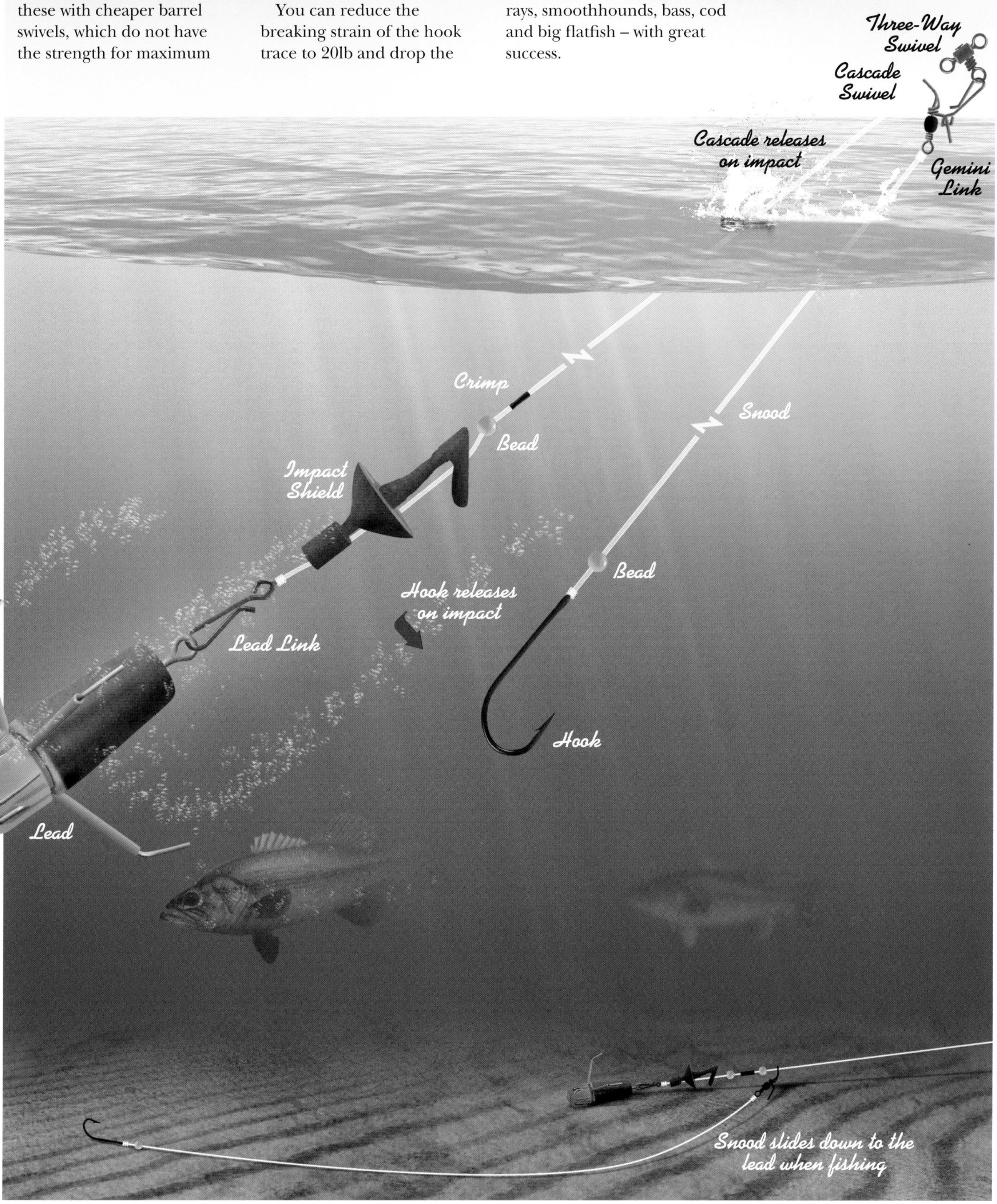

Three-Way Swivel

Cascade Swivel

Cascade releases on impact

Gemini Link

Crimp

Bead

Snood

Impact Shield

Hook releases on impact

Bead

Lead Link

Hook

Lead

Snood slides down to the lead when fishing

"Blimey!... Brilllllliaaaant!"

Watch "Brilliant"
www.youtube.com/fishinginfoukat

www.facebook.com/fishinginfouk
www.twitter.com/fishinginfouk

Find more, learn more, catch more at fishinginfo.co.uk the "Brilliant" new website from the Angling Trust

ANGLING TRUST   Environment Agency   Met Office   POST OFFICE

LOOP RIG

This two-hook version of Ian Golds' rig is handy when big fish are about.

History

This rig was reportedly developed by top match angler Ian Golds close to 20 years ago, and originally as a three-hook rig. In some quarters it's referred to as the 'Portsmouth rig' due to the area the rig was first designed for.

This version, though, has been modified to be a two-hook rig to increase overall casting range and to better suit freelance angling for more targeted species. The components used also signal the intent that this rig can be fished at maximum range, and will handle bigger fish if need be better than a standard match rig can.

How It Works

As you can see from the completed rig, it's very streamlined with minimal components to reduce air drag, ensuring that the rig flies to maximum range. With few components being used, the rig is also less likely to spook fish when fished in shallow, clear water.

The rig also rarely, if ever, tangles because the line and hooks release without problem when the lead weight hits the sea and the rig body falls slack on impact.

The obvious advantage with this rig is that the bottom hook trace is positioned tight behind the lead link. This puts the bait hard on the sea bed, but with natural movement from the flowing trace. This is the hook that's most likely to take dabs, flounders, plaice and rockling.

The top trace is more governed by being attached to the rig body. As surf or swells pass over the rig and up the line, the rig body will lift and fall in the water. So this top hook trace also has movement, but is more likely to lift up off the bottom occasionally. This offers a different type of bait presentation that will appeal more to round fish such as whiting, coalies, school bass, codling and pouting.

In calmer conditions it can pay to get the

Build Sequence

01 Start with a 48in length of 60lb clear-mono rig body and, to one end, tie on a Gemini rig clip.

02 Slide on a rig crimp, 3mm rig bead, size 10 rolling swivel and another bead and crimp, which will form the bottom snood. Crimp this in place just above the Gemini clip. Repeat the sequence once more for the top snood and leave loose for now.

03 Finish the main rig by tying on a size 4 rolling swivel as the main leader to the rig-attachment point.

04 The top hook snood is about 12 inches long and made from 20lb fluorocarbon or mono. Slide on a rubber stop and sequin and add a size 2 Aberdeen hook.

The bottom hook snood is also 20lb, but is in two sections. The first section that's tied to the bottom swivel is about eight to 14 inches long with a Cascade swivel tied to the free end by the big eye.

05 Now tie another 6in section of 20lb mono to the other end of the Cascade swivel, with a rubber stop, sequin and hook added.

06 To get the tension absolutely right on the bottom hook trace, hang the rig up with a lead weight attached. Position the lowest hook in the lead clip, add the top hook into the clip on the Cascade swivel, then slide the top swivel assembly up the rig until the hook snood comes just tight. Now crimp the top swivel assembly in place. The 6in section of the lowest hook snood is now tight inside the lead clip and the Cascade swivel holds the top hook snood straight. The longer 8in section of the bottom snood is slightly slack and forms the loop that the rig takes its original name from.

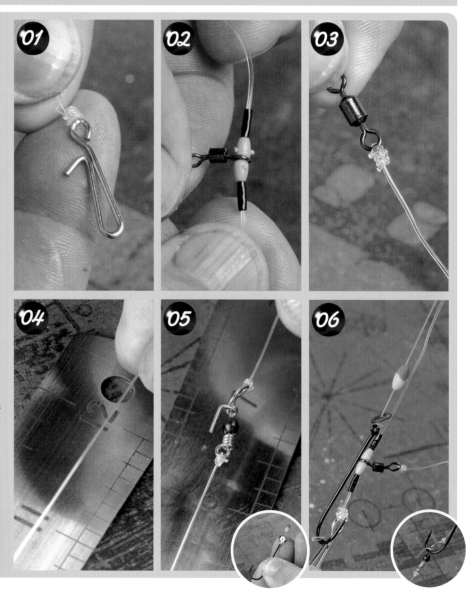

bottom hook further away from the lead weight to avoid spooking fish, but more importantly to add more movement to the bait in the flowing tide. To achieve this, simply lengthen the first section of the lowest hook snood out from eight to 14 inches. Extending this means that the loop size is increased when the hooklength is tight in the lead clip, but this is unimportant. Remember that only the end section from the Cascade swivel to the hook needs to stay the same to keep the lower and middle hook snoods tight when the hooks are clipped in.

When making the hooklengths it pays to use fluorocarbon rather than plain mono – there are various reasons why. Firstly, the fluorocarbon is more resistant to abrasion than plain mono when washing over sand, so you can use lighter hooklengths without the fear of abrasive nicks in the line's surface creating undue weakness. Being slightly stiffer, it also helps avoid tangles when fishing in among the surf tables when fishing very shallow water. It's also less easy for the fish to see and thereby become spooked by in clear water conditions.

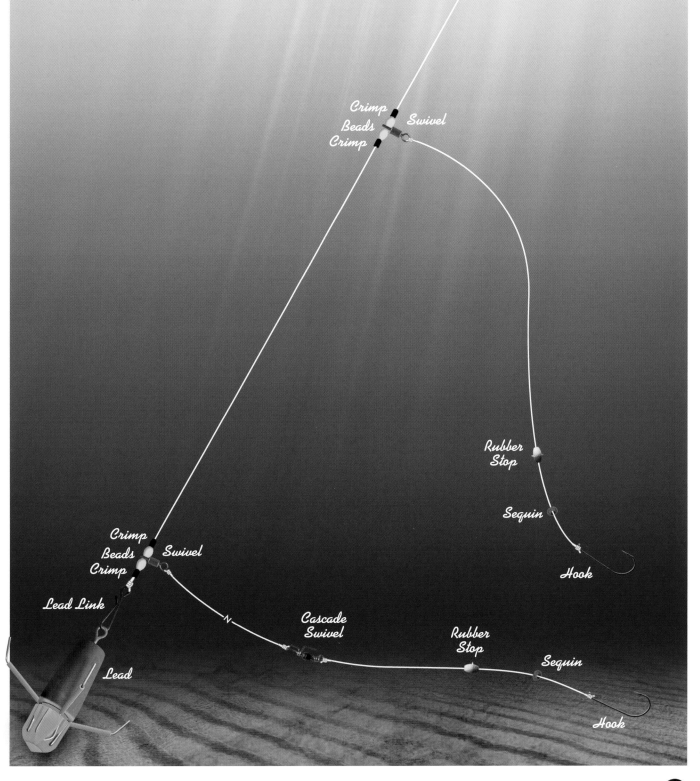

Swivel

Crimp
Beads
Crimp

Swivel

Rubber
Stop

Sequin

Hook

Crimp
Beads
Crimp

Swivel

Lead Link

Cascade
Swivel

Rubber
Stop

Sequin

Lead

Hook

BOMBER RIG

When you are limited to one rod, this rig covers a lot of bases.

History

A bomber rig will blow all other traces out of the water when it comes to casting small baits to maximum range. Many anglers believe that the rig was spawned from the original one-hook paternoster, but this is not the case. It was developed by several anglers realising the effectiveness of having two hooks fishing close together, along with the advantage of having both a long and short hooklength to vary bait presentation. Nobody can prove who the original instigator was, although many like to lay claim to it!

The rig is said to be a matchman's 'banker' rig at long range, when all else fails. The bomber is designed to achieve maximum range when using two small baits. This is due to its streamlined nature, with both baits being clipped, side-by-side, into the Impact Shield and flying through the dead air behind the shield to minimise the wind resistance.

How It Works

The bomber rig is traditionally chosen for fishing at medium-to-long range, but mostly long. It has the ability to present two different baits relatively close together to give single fish a choice, but also the two different baits can be used to tempt different types of fish. For example, you could have a mackerel strip for dogfish and whiting on one hook, and worm bait for flatfish on the other. This is why the rig is often referred to as the matchman's 'banker' rig, because it multiplies your chances of fish when you can only fish the one rig and need to be at maximum range.

Another benefit of this rig is that the shorter, lower hook trace will fish bait hard on the sea bed, and will target bottom feeders, such as flatfish. The top, longer trace will flutter and swing in the tide giving a more natural form of presentation and target fish feeding and swimming just up off the sea bed.

Some anglers choose to use the bomber rig with a small size 4 or 2 Aberdeen hook on the bottom hook trace for the smaller fish. They then go for a single 2/0 or 3/0 Viking pattern on the longer, top trace, fishing bigger worm or crab baits to target bass, cod and the like to cover their options.

When fishing at long range in shallow surf conditions, even at night, it's better to make the hook traces from fluorocarbon line, as it is stiffer than mono. This helps avoid any chance of the two hook traces tangling as the surf lifts over the rig and tumbles them around. In calm seas you can switch to softer and lighter clear monofilament lines to increase the natural movement of the baits.

The rubber rig stop and sequin act as a bait stop, preventing the bait from being blown back up the snood during a powerful cast due to air pressure. You

Build Sequence

01 Begin with 30 inches of 60lb or 80lb rig body mono and tie a Gemini lead link to one end.

02 Slide on a Breakaway Impact Shield followed by a 3mm bead and crimp. Leave around 1½ inches for the shield to slide in; this will avoid hook snood stretch during the cast.

03 Slide on a rig crimp, a 3mm rig bead, a size 10 rolling swivel, another bead and a crimp. Now repeat the sequence so that you have two sets of components ready for fixing to the rig body. Finish off the main rig body by tying on a size 4 rolling swivel.

04 Tie 12 inches of 25lb fluorocarbon line to the lower hook snood swivel.

05 Slide on a rubber rig stop and a sequin, then finish with a size 2 Aberdeen hook for smaller species, or 1/0 Viking hooks for bigger fish. Place the hook in the Impact Shield and slide the lowest snood crimp up the rig until the snood line comes just tight. Hold everything firm and crimp the trace swivel in position.

06 The top hook trace needs to be around 24 inches long with a stop and sequin threaded on. This is, again, positioned by placing the hook in the Impact Shield, sliding the swivel and crimp assembly up the line until the trace comes tight. Crimp this in place. Both hooks will sit in the Impact Shield for casting, but release when the lead hits the water.

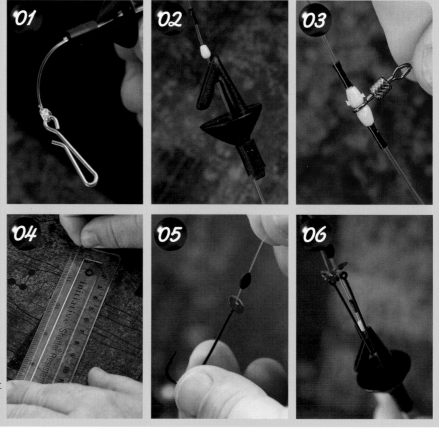

can substitute the sequin for two or three 5mm attractor beads in clear water. This can increase your chances of plaice and other flatfish. Alternatively, at night, replace the sequin with a couple of small luminous beads to advertise the bait visually to hunting fish.

Top Tips

01 When retrieving a bomber trace with no fish on, never reel in too quickly as the snoods can become tangled, especially as you draw it through the surf.

02 If using single hooks on the snoods, ensure that you use bait stops to prevent the bait from blowing back up the snood. This will dramatically cut casting distance and damage the bait.

03 You can also use Impact Leads instead of Impact Shields. If you choose to fish at extreme range, Impact Leads will be more effective.

04 When setting the hooks in the Impact Shield, put the bigger bait in first followed by the smaller one. Occasionally, if placing the smaller bait in the shield first, it can fail to eject from the shield's retaining arm.

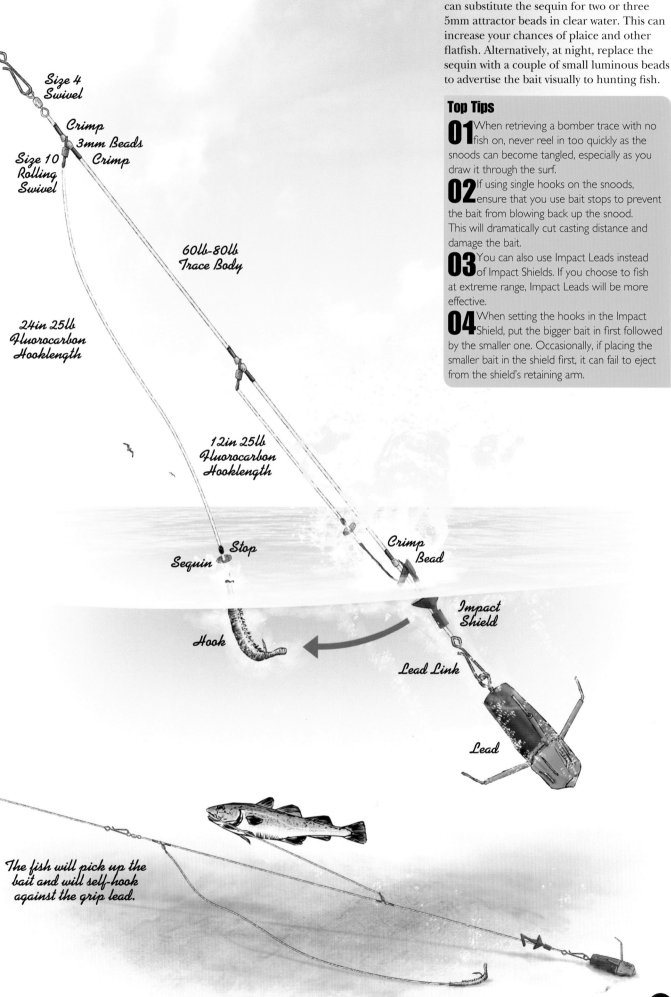

Size 4 Swivel

Crimp
3mm Beads
Crimp

Size 10 Rolling Swivel

60lb-80lb Trace Body

24in 25lb Fluorocarbon Hooklength

12in 25lb Fluorocarbon Hooklength

Sequin

Stop

Crimp Bead

Hook

Impact Shield

Lead Link

Lead

The fish will pick up the bait and will self-hook against the grip lead.

LONG-LINE RIG

A floating bead maximises bait movement and attraction on this rig.

History

This rig was introduced to the UK by Portuguese and Spanish shore anglers, and it's also popular throughout many Mediterranean countries for a whole host of smaller species. Its name there is unknown, but here it's been christened the 'long-line' rig because it vaguely resembles a commercial-fisherman's long line.

It uses very short hook links with float beads and has proved effective for targeting garfish, mackerel, bream, flatfish, gurnards and weevers, and will even take bass, dogfish, smelt, poor cod and pouting. The rig has also caught lots of small wrasse when fishing over rougher ground.

It's been kept fairly quiet, but some of the south-coast matchmen have been using this rig successfully over the past couple of summers in matches fished over shallower beaches. The rig has also caught on in Ireland but, again, the use of it is being kept quiet by competition anglers who have done well with it.

How It Works

This can be used for general shore fishing in shallow water where the length of the rig will spread the baits and cover more ground. The float beads will also lift smaller baits, such as maddie rag or small strips of lug, squid or mackerel up off the sea bed where they will flutter in the tide and attract fish.

The rig is also excellent when fished over any weed growth because the baits will sit on top of the weed and remain exposed – and when fishing into eelgrass beds because, again, the baits will be suspended up in the water.

It's important to understand that the gap between the float bead and the hook is only an inch or so. This maximises the buoyancy of the bait and doesn't put the fish off one jot.

The choice of sliding stops means that you can change the position of the snoods to suit the fish. If it's only the bottom hook that is catching, move the top two hooks further down, or vice versa.

The rig can be further adapted for selective conditions by making the rig body out of 20lb fluorocarbon and using just 6lb hooklengths when fishing calm, very shallow, gin-clear seas in daylight. Obviously the light rig body requires short casts using lead weights of no more than 2oz, with safety in mind.

You can also change the size of the float bead according to what you want the bait to do. Smaller beads and baits will see the bait just lift off the sea bed and attract flatfish and so on, but bigger beads will suspend smaller baits well up off the sea bed and attract shoal feeders such as bream, along with gurnards, weevers, school bass, poor cod and pout. Also, since the beads act as attractors, try alternating the colours and see if one specific colour catches more fish.

The versatility of this rig is that it also proves highly effective fished vertically from piers, jetties and breakwaters. The 7ft-plus length of the rig means that you can cover a good depth of the water column. The bottom hook will still attract the bottom feeders, but the middle and top hooks are more likely to catch mackerel, smelt, garfish and bream during slack water when they come up off the

Build Sequence

01 Take 90 inches of 60lb clear mono line for the trace and at one end tie on a Gemini lead link.

02 Cut a 5mm length of neoprene tubing, pass the trace line through the tubing, bring it back on itself and pass it through the tubing again. Pull the line tight to form a sliding stop knot. Now slide on a 3mm rig bead, a size 12 rolling swivel, another rig bead and add another neoprene tubing stop knot as before.

03 Repeat step two twice more to create three snood swivels.

04 Finish the main rig by tying on a size 4 rolling swivel.

05 The hooklengths are ideally 15lb fluorocarbon, or clear mono. Onto each of the hook snoods slide a medium-sized float bead, then add a rubber float stop.

06 Finish by tying on a size 6 Kamasan B940 Aberdeen hook.

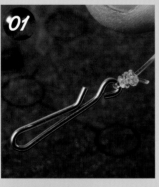

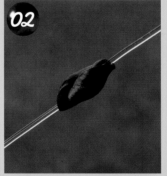

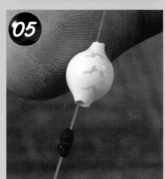

sea bed. Triggerfish will also take this rig when it's fished close to jetty supports, which isn't surprising.

The long-line rig should do well through the winter for flounders, dabs, whiting and school bass, especially during the scratching season early in the year when fish and bites are few and far between.

5mm of Neoprene Tubing

Size 12 Rolling Swivel

Beads

5mm of Neoprene Tubing

50lb Trace Body

Floating Bead

Rubber Stop

Size 6 Hook

Lead Link

Lead

Mark blasts a sandeel to range in search of turbot.

A Shore THING

Kev Gerry is forced to watch his pal, sea fishing expert Mark Williams, catch turbot from a Cornish shore mark after a tackle blunder.

The number of beaches capable of producing consistent turbot action has diminished alarmingly over the years, due to the commercial boys taking more than their fair share of these sought-after flatfish.

In fact, some shore marks that used to produce loads of sizeable turbot are now totally devoid of these stunning flatties – so finding somewhere to catch them is becoming ever trickier.

Fortunately my old mate Mark Williams, a member of the Royal Navy Sea Angling team and a regular in its tournament-casting squad, knows a few Cornish gems where the chances of catching a turbot are greatly increased.

The area he decided to take me to on my maiden turbot trip was a spot on the southwest side of Lizard Point, known as Church Cove. It sits right in front of the village of Gunwalloe – which is one of the first entries found in the Domesday Book – and is surrounded by a landscape designated an Area of Outstanding Natural Beauty.

But the cove, despite being a turbot hotspot, is probably best known for its 15th century church of St Winwaloe, which nestles on the cliff on the northern side of Church Cove and has a small, squat bell tower that's detached from the main place of worship and set into the solid rock.

Just reaching the mark is like turning back the clock several hundred years to an age when the folk living in the tiny surrounding hamlets carved out livings from tin mining or raising a few cattle to help make ends meet.

The area looked even more inviting as we stepped from Mark's car an hour before low water and into glorious sunshine, but it was as we started to unload our gear that a dark cloud was suddenly cast upon us… I had forgotten my rod!

I had driven from my Plymouth home over to Mark's house at Saltash before transferring my tackle to his motor – or at least I thought it had all been packed. It turned out that while I believed Mark had put my rod in the car he thought I had completed the task. And that's how my prized Century rod, which is my lucky charm, too, was left still standing up against the hedge at Mark's house as we drove away! It was now a case of a quick call to his wife to ask her to bring it safely inside, which, as it turned out, she had already done after spotting

Mark's preferred turbot rig: an up-and-over single-snood clipped down for long range.

the rod all on its lonesome. It was some consolation to discover that my favourite rod was at least safe, but the gloom quickly returned when I realised that I would need to use a rod that wasn't mine. This may seem a little superstitious but we have all got to believe in some luck, haven't we? So, to make the best of a bad job, I decided that at least I would be able to spend the day watching an expert at work and be able to pick up a few tips if his rod didn't work for me.

Sandy Hotspot

The mark has a huge sand bar that runs parallel to beaches each side of the rocks that we would be fishing from, and probably the reason it's so productive is that any large fishing boats are unable to access the area. This is due to the sand bar being so close to the shore, no more than 100 yards out. Also, at low water on a big spring tide you can just about see the top of the bar below the water and this is what makes the spot a bit of a hotbed for turbot, because feed gathers here.

The terrain is a kind of sandy shale, which turbot just adore because it just happens to be home to one of their favourite quarries… sandeels.

The rock formation we would be fishing →

A cracking little turbot of 1lb 2oz results from Mark's fourth cast.

from is accessible from either side from about half-tide down – the north side of the mark is Church Cove Beach, and the south side of the mark is Poldhu Beach. There are many platforms to fish from, along with plenty of room for pendulum casting to launch any streamlined baits out to the required range – I can cast quite a long way, but had no idea how my borrowed rod would fare…

Turbot Charged

So, without complaining about my situation we set about tackling up for the session ahead, and I just decided to watch this expert at large and how he goes about fishing for turbot for a few casts before wetting a line.

I have to admit that I have

Rig Choice

Mark's preferred rig for the session was a long up-and-over pulley Pennel; he favours this over most other rigs. The rig consisted of 60lb trace body with an 18lb hooklength, and he specifies that it's got to be clear line on both.

The sandeel was trimmed front and back then threaded onto a size 1/0 hook. Whereas I would whip mine on with bait elastic, Mark used the Pennel way of holding the bait on the first hook by winding the upper hook, a size 2/0, around the trace line three or four times and then hooking it into the tail end of the eel. This is a way of securing the bait and preventing it from sliding up the trace line when casting out; it also gives the angler a chance of presenting a decent bait with two points for hooking.

always been totally unaware of any marks in the southwest where you can actually target just turbot. I have caught them from the shore in the past but only by chance and to be fair I don't know any other anglers who could set out with purely turbot in mind. Mark has fished since the age of 10 and

has grown up casting from the south and north coastlines of Cornwall.

Action Stations

After tackling up Mark revealed his favourite and must-have turbot bait – sandeels. They can be frozen or fresh dead, and even alive if you can get

them. His were fresh dead from the day before, kept well refrigerated overnight, and then transferred to a cool box for the trip down, which is vital when it's a baking-hot day.

Up Against The Bar…

Mark's next step was to select which side of the bar that he wanted to cast to, explaining that he preferred the left-hand side because it drops off rapidly and has brought him the most success in the past. Although he hadn't fished this particular spot for two years, some things in fishing rarely alter and he was pretty confident as he belted his clipped-down rig out about 120 yards and then slowly wound in until he felt resistance when his lead came up behind the bar. After he had made three casts, I tried

Even small turbot have big mouths – they are keen hunters.

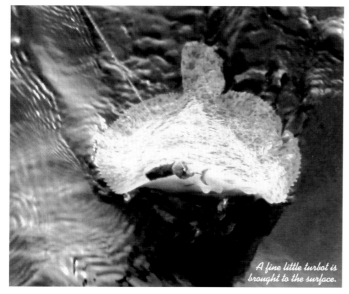

A fine little turbot is brought to the surface.

to do the same, though with a strange rod I didn't get so far first cast – I really didn't feel confident.

Rat-A-Tat-Tat

It took just four casts and less than an hour before he had the first telltale sign of a bite. This was a slight tug on the rod tip then a nice sharp pull-down followed by slack line – pretty much like a ray bite only not as violent. Mark was quick to point out that he fishes for turbot in exactly the same way that he does for flounders in the winter: when a bite shows on the rod he gives it time to develop, to enable the fish to engulf the sandeel, which is

not as soft as baits such as lug and rag that flatfish find easy to swallow. By allowing the bite to develop you reduce the risk of pulling the bait out of the turbot's mouth.

Mission Accomplished

After a few minutes Mark picked the rod up and started feeling for any movement on the business end. The moment he detected a slight tug at the end he lifted the rod and started to wind slowly to be sure of setting the hook. I was standing slightly above him as he reeled the fish in and was the first to see that he had indeed succeeded in hitting his target species with →

When at range, after a bite, you must then feel for the fish to be sure that it has taken the bait properly before lifting into it.

How Mark Williams Baits Up With Sandeel For Turbot...

01 Begin with a Pennel-hook setup and as good a quality eel as you can get.

02 Cut off the eel's head and tail.

03 You are left with a juicy body full of scent.

04 Enter the hook point in at one end of the eel.

05 Thread the hook through the body carefully, being sure not to pierce or split the eel.

06 Job done: one intact eel body with the hook passed through it.

07 Wind the line three times around the top hook and pass it through the eel as pictured.

08 Clip the hook into the impact shield and you're ready to blast your sandeel to long range!

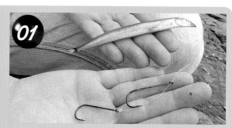

The beaches nearby get busy, and water sports can sometimes interrupt the fishing.

his first fish. It wasn't a huge turbot at 1lb 2oz but it got him off the mark and was quickly returned after a couple of photographs were taken.

Mark blasted another offering to the horizon before we continued chatting. It was then that I noticed that there were guys in fishing kayaks about 400 yards out in front of us and after watching them for a while we could see that they were also bringing up fish that looked very much like turbot.

High Hopes

Although Mark's initial turbot was on the small side, Church Cove is a well-known rock mark that can produce some very decent catches. His personal best from the area is a very respectable 5lb 1oz landed three years ago. You might think that that's not very big, but I would say it's a tidy size from the shore given the way our fish stocks of 'all species' appear to be diminishing as the years go by. There are also some decent small-eyed rays to be had when autumn approaches.

Seconds Out, Fish Two!

Mark's rod showed another bite as it started nodding furiously – something we hadn't initially noticed because we were still peering at the kayak guys. Mark went through the same process of ensuring that the fish had taken the bait properly before winding in another small but beautiful

turbot; its mottled-browny coloration clearly visible as it came through the water. It was easy to see that if you laid the fish on the sea bed it would be difficult to spot due to the way it blended perfectly with the fine shingle bottom.

Some may feel that two small turbot were hardly

worth the effort, but it was still certainly more than I caught, and there is some real satisfaction to be gained by setting out with a particular species in mind and then hitting the target. I just wish that my rod had been at my side – rather than stood up in Mark's hallway.

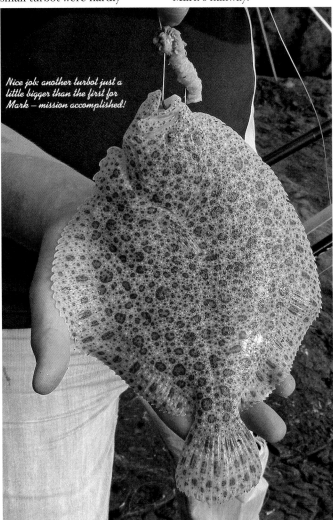

Nice job: another turbot just a little bigger than the first for Mark – mission accomplished!

Notable Facts

01 This mark is accessible from the road above and from both the beaches either side.

02 Long pulley rigs or long up-and-overs work well here.

03 Sandeels and strips of fresh or frozen mackerel work best here for the turbot and rays later in the year.

04 Casting to the left of the sand bar is preferred.

05 Church Cove is a well-known local mark and can get quite busy in the summer months.

06 You can park in the public car park all day and it's not expensive.

07 As far as directions go, simply drive to Helston in Cornwall, then take the B3297 for four-and-a-half miles to Gunwalloe.

08 On both Church Cove and Poldhu Beaches the bass fishing at night in the late summer months can be very productive.

Long-And-Low
SHORE RIG

Keeping the hook bait away from the lead is easy with this rig, which is very effective for rays.

History

The modern concept of the long-and-low rig has been around since the mid 1970s. It's a rig that never gets the publicity it deserves, yet it's one of the most popular with the more experienced anglers when targeting winter cod, rays, and big autumnal bass.

The rig you're about to tie has been simplified, and now uses minimal rig components to minimise drag in the air during the cast for maximum casting range, but also to limit any potential tackle loss and keep costs down when fishing over mixed and rough ground.

How It Works

With both the hook and the hook trace positioned correctly in the clips, during the cast the hook trace will stay secure and remain streamlined to aid casting distance. When the lead weight hits the sea, both the hook and trace will fall free of the clips, which will see the trace flow out in the tide as the rig settles on the sea bed.

Being positioned close behind the lead weight and being on a long flowing trace, the bait is now free to move on the sea bed with the flow of the tide and any surf movement. This creates a very natural, free-roaming presentation. Equally, the bait will be fishing hard on the sea bed, exactly where big predators such as winter cod, summer rays and bass are searching for the majority of their food.

It's a recurring theme with modern rigs, but although mono line for the hook trace is okay, it's better to use fluorocarbon. The reason being is that fluorocarbon is slightly stiffer, and is therefore less prone to tangling when in moving water. But it's also more resistant to abrasion from teeth and general wear and tear. In fact, you can use a lighter breaking strain – say 30lb instead of 40lb or even 50lb mono –to increase the movement of a bait.

Although there are several alternatives as to how you rig the top hook, the simple method of wrapping the line around the shank of the top

Build Sequence

01 Begin with 36 inches of 60lb clear mono and, at one end, tie on a Gemini rig clip.

02 Slide on a rig crimp, 3mm bead, size 6 rolling swivel, another bead and a crimp. Leave these loose for now.

03 At the free end, tie on an inverted Gemini bait clip.

04 The hook trace is about 60 inches of 50lb fluorocarbon or clear mono. Tie this to the free end of the swivel.

05 To the remaining end of the hook trace, slide on a size 4/0 Mustad 79510 hook, then tie on a size 4/0 Mustad Viking 79515 hook. Wrap the line around the shank of the top hook three times to secure it in place.

06 Place the bottom hook in the bent clip of the lower Gemini link. Put the hooklength inside the clip of the inverted Gemini link, now slide the crimp and swivel assembly down the rig-body line until it comes just tight, and crimp in place.

TopTip

To achieve the correct hooklength tension, place a lead in the bottom lead link and then hang the trace via the top link. Now loop the snood over the top link and place the hook in the bottom link. Pull the crimps and swivel downwards until the hooklength becomes tight, then crimp in place.

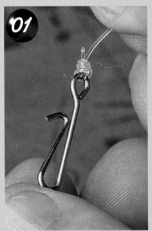

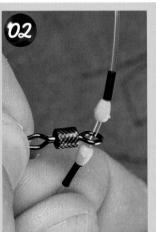

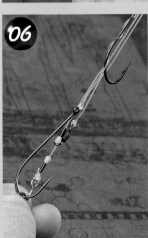

hook is easy and effective. But, more so, it means that you can instantly adjust the position of the hook to accommodate bigger or smaller baits by simply unwrapping the line, repositioning the hook and winding it back up again.

This rig also encourages self-hooking by the fish. With the trace positioned tight behind the lead and the trace flowing out in the tide, as a fish takes the bait it invariably does so by approaching the bait from downtide as it follows up the scent trail. As it takes the bait it will then turn back to swim with the tide – and, as it does so, it will come up hard against the grip lead, which will help set the hook.

Another advantage of this rig is that when a fish is hooked, the lead weight is lifted upwards above the fish. This keeps it away from the worst of snags and helps reduce fish and tackle loss when fishing over mixed and rough ground.

Although effective as a long-range casting rig on surf beaches and in shallow water, this rig is also perfect when casting short to medium range into deep water, because the bait is guaranteed to be hard on the sea bed. If you fish a conventional paternoster rig into deep water and have a tight line, then often the hook trace is often not effectively fishing hard on the bottom. This affects presentation and can seriously limit the number of bites you get.

Inverted Lead Link

Swivel

Crimp
Beads
Crimp

Swivel

Hook

Hook

Lead Link

Lead

THE 180 RIG

Boost your bite indication with this rig from angling legend Mike Thrussell.

History

Sea angling legend Mike Thrussell probably invented this rig – although others experimented with the basic design just as he did – and he has been using it for nearly 20 years.

However, it's certainly not one he has seen being used by many other anglers on the beach.

The rig is taken from the basic 'long-and-low' design, but inverted so that the hook trace and bait come back in a 180-degree direction when in position on the ready-to-cast rig. Hence the name… the 180 rig!

Due to the clipped-in position of the bait, the rig is ideal for close to medium-range casting and is especially effective when fished into deep water such as off breakwaters, steep beaches and rock ledges onto clean sand or mixed rough ground.

How It Works

Mike Thrussell came up with this rig to maximise bite detection in deeper water and to give the bait the freedom to move in the tide but still be hard on the sea bed. This is something that the long-and-low rig, which would be the typical choice in a deep-water situation, is not as effective at achieving, with the fish needing to fully take the bait and swim away, pulling the lead out to register a bite on the rod tip.

You'll see that the hook trace is roughly twice the length of the rig body. This guarantees that the bait is rolling around on the sea bed to maximise any tidal movement, and give natural presentation.

You'll also notice that the hook trace is tied just below the connector swivel. This means that the rig is more sensitive at registering bites than a conventional long-

and-low rig designed to fish the bait and hook trace flat on the sea bed when the line is fished tight to the lead. On the 180 rig, even a shy bite from a small whiting will register on the rod tip.

The Sakuma sliding crimp is important positioned below the inverted bait clip. This needs to grip the rig-body line semi-tight, but be able to slide slightly under pressure. If the crimp slides too easily, then the bait will eject prematurely in mid-cast, though at short range this is not a problem. Ideally the crimp should be crimped just tight enough to move fractionally under normal casting pressure. Having the crimp sliding under pressure prevents the hook trace from stretching and extending the hook-trace length beyond the inverted bait clip, plus it gives

Build Sequence

01 Begin with 40 inches of 60lb/80lb rig-body line. To one end tie on a Gemini lead clip link.

02 Slide on a Sakuma sliding rig crimp, a 3mm rig bead and an inverted bait clip. Crimp the bait clip in place 30 inches above the Gemini lead link, but don't secure the crimp solidly; squeeze it so that it will just about slide on the rig-body line.

03 Slide on a rig crimp, a 3mm rig bead, a size 8 rolling swivel, another bead and a rig crimp. Leave these loose for now.

04 Finish the rig with a size 4 rolling swivel. Crimp the hook trace swivel assembly in place one inch below the size 4 connector swivel.

05 The hook trace is 60 inches – longer if you want – of 30lb/40lb fluorocarbon or clear mono line. Add a short section of neoprene tubing or Powergum stop knot, then a sequin to act as a bait stop.

06 The hook is usually a single size 4/0 Kamasan B940 or a Mustad Viking 79515 – this can also be made as a two-hook Pennel rig.

To ready the rig for casting, put the hook trace into the bottom bait clip, bring the hook upwards towards the top of the trace and clip the hook into the inverted bait clip using the sliding feature of the Sakuma rig crimp to fully tighten the hook trace for casting.

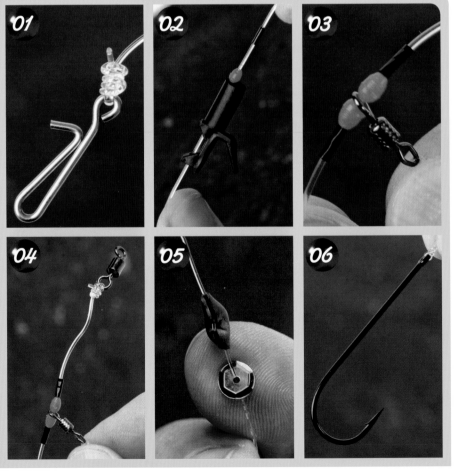

perfect release when casting further.

Mike uses this rig mainly for bass and cod in deeper-water situations, but with the bait on the sea bed it will also take huss, rays and strap congers, plus he uses a lighter version when plaice fishing into deep-water channels at close range with the line almost vertical into the water with great effect.

The rig has also proved effective in the past off the peat ledges east of Newport in South Wales.

Swivel

Crimp

Beads

Swivel

Crimp

Hook

Sequin

Stop

60lb-80lb Trace Body

60in of 30lb-40lb Clear Mono

Water pressure will release the line from the clip

Gemini Clip-Down Lead Link

Lead

The 60in snood will allow the rig to fish perfectly in deep water

Two-Hook
POP-UP RIG

Floating beads can help keep your baits away from detritus and pesky crabs.

History

Carp anglers think that they invented the pop-up rig – but not so! Sea anglers were using bits of cork above hooks to lift baits up off the sea bed to both avoid crab activity and to add movement to baits well over a century ago!

Sea pop-up rigs were somewhat forgotten, though, until the introduction of float beads in the mid-1980s. This rebirth was brought about by some of the UK's top freelance and competition anglers, who were looking to increase catches of smaller fish in both calm, clear sea conditions, but especially when fishing over and into weed beds.

This particular two-hook rig was developed for targeting black bream off the North Wales coast. But, along with bream it also proved adept at catching dabs, flounders, pouting, poor cod, eels, small pollack, wrasse and garfish.

How It Works

This rig is designed to fish small baits popped up above shallow blanket weed, which can otherwise smother and hide normal legered baits. It also suspends bait up in the water between weed stems to target fish hunting through the weed.

The beads move in the tide flow adding natural movement, which will increase the number of bites.

Get A-Float

For smaller single, or two or three maddie rag baits, one large-size float bead will be enough to suspend the bait up in the water. Bigger baits such as mackerel and squid strips and small sections of king rag and lug may require two float beads.

For fish feeding on, or just off, the sea bed, a hooklength of between 10 and 15 inches is

Build Sequence

01 Begin with 40 inches of 60lb clear mono and, at one end, tie on a Gemini lead link.

02 Slide on a rig crimp, 3mm rig bead, size 10 swivel, another rig bead and a crimp. Repeat this process for the second snood. Leave these loose for the time being.

03 Complete the rig body by tying on a size 4 rolling swivel.

04 Crimp the first trace swivel in place 12 inches above the lead link. The second trace swivel needs crimping in place at 32 inches above the lead link.

05 The hook traces are made from 15lb fluorocarbon or clear mono. The lowest hook trace is 10 inches long, while the top hook trace is 14 inches long, but this can be up to 32 inches if you want to fish higher up into mid-water.

06 Onto each hooklength slide a rubber rig stop, then one or two very buoyant float bead/s depending on the size of bait being used, followed by another rubber rig stop.

07 Hooks for this rig vary between size 2 and 8, but are generally size 6 Kamasans or size 4 B940 Aberdeens.

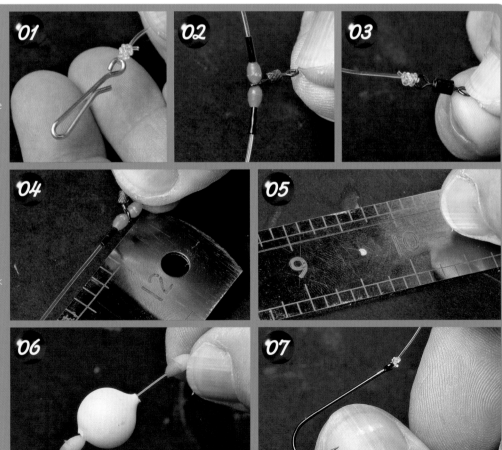

perfect, as the bait presents itself either in front of them or just above them. As an example, flatfish have no problem rising up off the sea bed to take suspended bait.

Depth

However, you need to consider the depth of any blanket weed and adjust the length of the hook trace accordingly, to ensure that the bait sits up above the weed in a free state. Equally, the top hooklength can be increased to be up to 30 inches or more, and fish bait in the mid and upper water column depending on the depth. This targets garfish, mackerel, pollack, wrasse and even bass.

Although having the float beads tight in behind the hook can work well enough, it often improves catches if the beads are positioned two to three inches away from the hook. This gives the bait more freedom to move, and, again, can dramatically improve the bite ratio on the day. This is especially so with black bream! The rig uses sliding rig stops, so that instant repositioning of the float bead is possible. Experiment on the day to find out exactly what the fish want.

Go Light

If bites are slow, try changing the breaking strain of the hooklength. Sometimes,

especially in clear, shallow water, the recommended 15lb line can be too heavy in diameter. Changing to lighter 10lb, or even 8lb, line can make a huge difference to the number of bites you get. This is the reason why fluorocarbon is used, because this is less easy for the fish to see compared with standard mono.

Delicate

Even the weight of the hook can affect catches, and by dropping down to a size 8, or even a size 10 in really clear, shallow, still conditions, the reduced weight gives the bait more natural movement that may induce a bite.

Critical Balance

As in carp fishing, sometimes the balance of bait can be critical too. Selecting a bead and bait size that sees it just lift and drop occasionally in the tide as it sways over the sea bed can be deadly for fish that otherwise show little interest. It pays, therefore, to carry a selection of float-bead sizes and, again, experiment.

Colours

Float-bead colour choice can also make a difference – a mix of blue and white works well for flounders and bream. Plaice like yellow beads split up by red or black. Garfish seem to like baits presented in front of blue and white or all-white beads. The smaller silver-coloured beads that are available can pick up smaller pouting and poor cod, and eels seem to favour these too.

Swivel

Crimp
Swivel
Beads
Crimp

Crimp
Swivel
Beads
Crimp

Stop
Floating Bead
Stop
Hook

Stop
Stop
Floating Bead
Hook

Lead Link

Lead

Bass On LURES

Ace boat angler and charter skipper **Glen Milligan** looks at how to become a great boat angler as he targets bass on lures…

Bass epitomise UK sea angling sport, and can offer some of the most exciting action available. They're hard fighting, tenacious and crafty – so you'll need to use your wits to try and outsmart them.

Provided you have balanced tackle – which basically means using a rod, reel, line and lure to match the size of the fish you target – they will always pull your string!

Arguably, the most testing way to catch them is with artificials and, for this feature, my goal is to guide you as best I can through the wonderful world of lure fishing.

About Bass

They are shoal fish and tend to swim with others similar to their own size – only occasionally do the larger fish mix with the smaller ones.

Bass →

Tides

Bigger tides with good runs are, in my opinion, the best for bassing, whether drifting over wrecks or broken ground. It's the disturbance in the water that draws out food items and prey fish, which send the bass into feeding mode.

This fine 4lb-plus bass fell for a Savage sandeel.

are pretty much armour plated with big, heavy-duty scales covering all the body. This is so that they can target and attack prey anywhere they wish, with no danger of damaging their skin. They have a series of eight to nine razor-sharp spines on the dorsal fin, as well as three protective spines at the anal fin, and a single spine at each pelvic fin. The gill covers also have razor-sharp edges so, when handling these fish, always be aware of these areas to avoid injury. A good tip is to wrap the fish in a wet towel when removing hooks until you become used to handling them with confidence.

Their colour varies depending on what grounds they're living and feeding over. On sand they tend to have backs of light grey to grey-green with silver sides and white bellies, and over reefs, rocks and mussel beds they are a darker blue, almost slate blue, on the back.

They can be caught from all around our coastline and generally breed from late January through to late May in deep water offshore.

Tackle

We all want to catch that magical double-figure fish, but the reality is that this doesn't happen very often and fish in the 4lb to 8lb bracket are more common. To this end, I prefer to use a light setup to enjoy the very best sport from the fish – although if a big one is hooked I can still bring it in on the gear. Suggestions are spinning rods, dedicated bass rods, light boat rods rated at

A simple running leger, with no boom or beads and only a long tag end to protect the knots, is Glen's favoured rig.

The trace is finished off with a Savage sandeel – Glen's new lure of choice!

A bite will either be a savage crash or a series of taps before the fish fully takes the lure – the secret is NOT to strike!

8lb to 12lb class and uptiders.

Couple these rods with a 5000 or 6000-size multiplier, or equivalent-size fixed-spool reel, and load them with 10lb to 15lb line. I prefer braid because I can get way more sport with this non-stretch

material and all the fight is brought to the rod and reel. But be sure to attach a mono or fluorocarbon leader of 10 feet or so to help prevent abrasion and to absorb the harder pulls and dives from a feisty fish!

Rigged Up

The rig we use is possibly the most simple we can, because all you do is slide a drilled bullet lead up your leader, tie on a swivel and then a 6ft length of trace line (preferably fluorocarbon to stay invisible to the fish) to your lure – simple! A great tip is to leave the tag ends of the knots long – because this will help to protect the knot from the lead constantly banging against it, without the need to use a bead.

You can, if you so desire, choose to jazz the rig up by trapping the lead between two swivels (with protective 5mm beads either side of it) on a 6in to 10in section of line – one swivel is tied to the leader and the other to the trace and lure.

I saw that our feature photographer, top angler Barney Wright, favoured this method, although I like to keep things really simple! He feels that he has more control and the fish hook themselves better as the lead will come up against resistance from the beads and drive the hook home. We both caught the same amount of fish during this trip, with neither of us missing bites, so it's simply down to personal choice.

Technique

Now that you're all tackled up, I will explain the technique we use to catch bass. We need to know the grounds where the bass are feeding and, in this instance, it's a series of banks where, for 90 per cent of the time, the fish are lying in wait for passing prey on the downtide edge of it. Firstly we hit tried-and-tested areas, but if nothing's there we'll move

Leader   Bead   Bead   Swivel
Swivel
Drilled-
Bullet Lead
Trace Line
Lure

Barney's Bass Drift Rig

on in search of the fish. They could be holding anywhere within these grounds, so a series of drifts are made and, when we find them, it's then up to me to stay in contact with the shoal!

The trace is lowered to the sea bed slowly, to avoid tangling, and soon you'll feel the lead touch the bottom. Let it drag for a few moments to settle, because the tide might demand more line – or sometimes less. But the art is to fish with the lead occasionally tapping the bottom and not dragging – this will lead to snagging up for sure!

That's another reason why I love braid, as you can feel everything and therefore fish more effectively. What actually happens is that your lead hits bottom, you reel up a turn or two, and then it's your lure/jighead you feel popping along the sea bed. This puts you right in the feeding zone, and it's now a question of whether you're using the right lure for the day. More about this later…

The Take!

A bite will either be a savage crash or a series of taps before the fish fully takes the lure – the secret is NOT to strike! When you do feel a take, resist striking, because you'll simply pull the lure unnaturally away from the fish and scare it off. Wait until your rod hoops over and then simply retrieve slowly for a couple of turns. Only strike when you're sure that the fish is on, to be sure the hooks are driven home into the bass' bony mouth. Make sure your drag is set correctly and it's game on!

Slowly does it…
Glen lowers the trace down
slowly to prevent tangles.

Touchy Feely…
After the lead hits the bottom, Glen
feels for it 'popping' on the sea bed
and tries to fish just off it.

While playing a bass, if the line goes slack and you think that you have lost the fish, I advise you to wind as fast as you can, because the fish is likely to be swimming at you fast!

In Session… Lures – The Savage Attack!

Bass can be really fussy and irritate the hell out of you by often going for different lures every day! Generally, though, the blue and white Sidewinders have served me extremely well here, but on this day the fish weren't so interested – we sent down white lures, orange, rhubarb and custard, mackerel imitations, Red Gills of all

Glen's Quickfire Lucky Seven Tips

01 If a lure isn't working, change it!

02 Braided line offers the best sport, but be sure to add a 10ft mono leader.

03 Use the lightest tackle you can for the best sport.

04 Never strike at the initial take – simply retrieve slowly for a few moments and then hit it!

05 If you're new to handling bass, wear gloves or wrap them in a damp towel when unhooking.

06 Return as many bass as you can – just keep enough for you and your family.

07 Always listen to the skipper!

varieties and, incredibly, the bass weren't tempted. We even tried livebait with little success – I almost began to think that there were no bass present.

Luckily, Barney had some Savage lures on board, which I hadn't used before and was keen to give a try. I have heard good reviews about this gear – these are basically fish and eel imitations that you fish off a jighead, and the one I used was a Savage sandeel, which looks perfect and also has a paddle-tail to act as an attractor. This lure was brilliant and accounted for several bass, which started the ball rolling; the others soon followed suit – Barney could only look on as he saw his lure collection rapidly deplete! →

Savage lures
A small selection from the Savage range – the slim eels can be fished straight on a hook and without a jighead if desired.

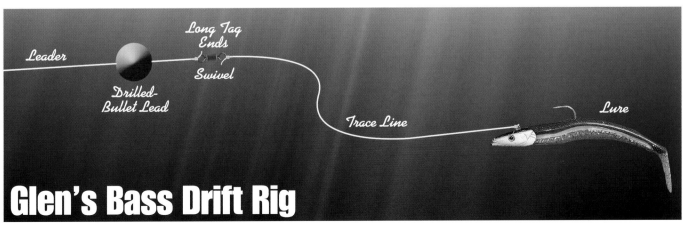

Glen's Bass Drift Rig

Leader

Drilled-Bullet Lead

Long Tag Ends

Swivel

Trace Line

Lure

He also had some new eel-shaped versions, which look superb, and these too are fished either using a jighead or a special hook that you can attach small lead shot to. This is because the lures actually float, so you can add weight to make them fish at almost any position on or above the sea bed. Quite how you can know exactly what depth they're fishing at, I don't know – unless you have an underwater video camera!

As Barney hadn't got many lead heads with him, I simply popped one onto a plain 4/0 hook and sent it down, where my drilled-bullet lead popped along the sea bed or just above, with the lure in tow during the drift. I knew the eel would be floating above the sea bed because there was no small weight attached and, as my trace was around six feet long, I suspect it fished roughly three feet from the bottom, taking into consideration the tide flow. For some reason, the bass couldn't resist these either – as soon as we popped them on, fish were boated every drift!

During The Murky Times...

The only downside to fishing with lures is when there's a sandy bottom on a strong tide, because the water can dirty up quickly and lures become ineffective. This is when livebaiting works best, or maybe some kind of attractor attached to the lure to grab the fishes' attention. Bass are drawn to disturbance, especially a wounded fish, so go for a lure that mimics the erratic motion of an injured prey fish.

Savage lures accounted for all the fish, with this sandeel being most deadly!

Bass will certainly put a good bend in your rod!

LIVE AID!

A fine pollack for Keith Mitchell, executive chef at The Grand Hotel, Eastbourne.

Barney Wright shows you how to take advantage of a situation when fish are literally showing you what they're feeding on.

It's a fact that below the waves carnage is occurring every day. Big fish are feeding on smaller fish, even smaller fish are picking up leftovers and the crabs are finishing the job off! This is known as the food chain, which we can exploit for our own gains.

How many times have you caught a good-sized fish when, as you go to take the hook out, it coughs up the remains of what it's been feeding on – usually baitfish, crabs or shellfish?

Those regurgitated morsels should give you a huge clue as to what bait you should be using, but not many anglers take heed of this. After all, this is what it has fed on in its natural environment and is also what it has been actively seeking. Sadly, many of us just carry on using the bait or lure that we had that fish on, and pay no thought to what's been brought to our attention. Well this is when you can really bag up!

Predatory!

The most common species that fall for this trick are bass, cod and pollack – of which the latter will be the star of this piece, because it was aboard *Carrick Lee* out of Newhaven while wrecking for cod and pollack using lures that the ideal scenario to use natural resources arose.

I was with fellow angler Simon Everett when a nice pollack was hauled up, which promptly regurgitated several live herring.

Cooking Up A Plan

It was Keith Mitchell, the executive chef at The Grand Hotel in Eastbourne, who had this fine fish, which was around the 5lb mark. It had taken a lure fished on a long, flowing trace, which it homed in on while taking a break from stuffing its face with the small baitfish. As it came over the rail, several live herring spilled from its mouth and onto the deck. Keith had the foresight to collect them and pop them straight into a bucket of fresh seawater, where they would happily stay alive for a couple of hours. He planned to use these instead of lures on the very next drift.

To Be Sure...

Usually, livebait is lip-hooked so it stays alive longer, but Keith had other plans because he knew that using this method often resulted in the bait working its way free, leaving you fishing with no bait and being none the wiser until you retrieve.

Keith's method is to use a size 4/0 fine-wire hook, and mount the herring by putting the hook in through its mouth and out through the top of its head, then binding it on firmly with bait elastic. The fish do not survive so long, but in all the confusion and carnage going on down below, he could be sure that the pollack would find his bait and hook! After all, if they're taking plastic lures, a fresh herring will be much tastier. The reality is that many of the best lures are made to be as realistic as possible in order to fool the fish, so what could be better than the real thing?

Proof Of The Pudding...

Using the same setup as before, but with bait instead of a plastic lure, Keith sent down exactly what the pollack were feasting on and I wasn't surprised to notice that he was immediately into a fish just

Snagged!

Very often it's the leads that become snared in a wreck, especially if you hook a big fish that swims the rig straight into it! But a great way to avoid this is to attach the lead to your rig via a weak link. This can be a lower breaking-strain line to your running line, or even a small elastic band. These will break before your line will and, therefore, allow you to retrieve your trace and bait/lure, along with, hopefully, a fish.

as the skipper told us we were right over the wreck. This was to inform us to slowly retrieve rigs up to just touch the top of the structure, then lower them back down as we passed by. This method puts bait as near to the fish-holding area as possible and, therefore, offers the best chance of hooking a fish. Snagging up is often inevitable, but the closer you get, the better – you've gotta be 'in it to win it'! →

Predatory fish simply cannot resist livebait.

Rigged Up

The rigs for wrecking are very simple. You basically fish a long, flowing trace attached to either a running-leger, Portland or flying-collar rig. Each of these rigs will present the lures/bait perfectly, but it's down to individual choice as to which one to use. However, when it comes to livebait, the best of the rigs is the Portland, because it's adjustable and allows the fish to swim up and down quite freely but only at the depth that YOU want it to!

Running-Leger Rig

Boom
Swivel
Bead
Hook
Lead

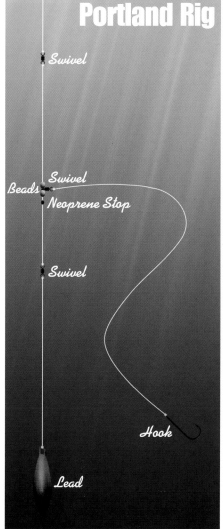

Portland Rig

Swivel
Beads
Swivel
Neoprene Stop
Swivel
Hook
Lead

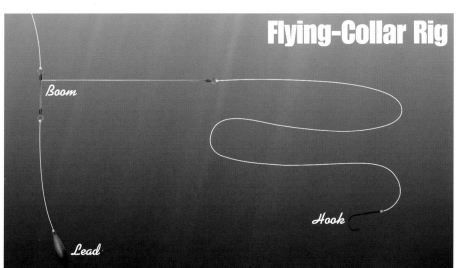

Flying-Collar Rig

Boom
Hook
Lead

Fish will often cough up what they've recently eaten, in this case herring – and still alive!

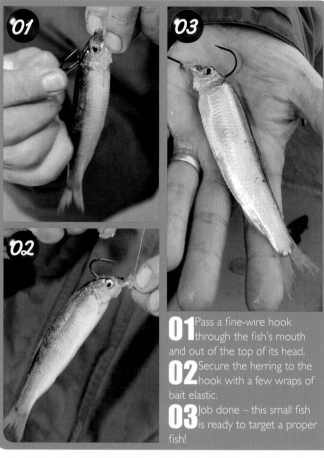

One A Drop!

While Simon and I continued to fish using lures and catching on every other drift or so, Keith was pulling up one on every drop! This, for me, conclusively proved that targeting fish with exactly what they're feeding on is a winning formula. The only problem was that Keith soon ran out of bait! The herring shoal had either moved away from the area or had been demolished – I felt that the latter was the most likely…

Good Imitation

I rummaged through my lure collection in an attempt to find something that looked as close to a herring as possible. I found a couple that fitted the bill and caught a couple of fish, although by the time I had a chance to use them in earnest, the tide was changing and the drifts slowing – and eventually we came to a standstill at slack water. This was when the pouting came on the feed, as they feel safe to come out of the wreck because the big predators move up in the water column to rest.

We didn't catch any more pollack, but the hectic action that Keith had enjoyed was proof enough that if you can discover what the fish are feeding on and present a live offering to them, the chances of a bumper haul are vastly increased.

01 Pass a fine-wire hook through the fish's mouth and out of the top of its head.

02 Secure the herring to the hook with a few wraps of bait elastic.

03 Job done – this small fish is ready to target a proper fish!

Keith lifts into one of several pollack caught using live herring.

Sponsored by Escape Watersports and Palm Equipment

THE ONLY OFFICIAL KAYAK FISHING CLUB IN THE UK

The largest kayak fishing club in the UK, founded in 2009

- With members from all over the UK, we are not restricted to Wales

- Meet in the Loughor Boating Club on the last Tuesday of each month

- We train with the RNLI at least once a year and are at the forefront of pushing safety in our sport and run regular safety, VHF radio and paddling courses

- We hold the largest kayak fishing competition in Europe along with two large freshwater kayak fishing competitions

SWKA presents the annual Oxwich Kayak Fishing Competition
Saturday 23rd July 2016
Oxwich Bay on the Gower Peninsula
Visit our website for all the latest details

Find us on Facebook: **South Wales Kayak Anglers (SWKA)**

WWW.SWKA.ORG.UK

Dab Two-Hook BOOM RIG

This rig will catch a wealth of species, but it's particularly suited to dabs and other flatfish – great on a species hunt!

History

We can't find any link back in time as to exactly how this rig came about, but it must stem from the brass booms that were so popular with sea anglers around the turn of the 20th century through to pre- and even post-World War II days.

Although most sea anglers board boats with bigger fish in mind these days, many do enjoy an hour or two dab bashing. Plus, with competition fishing mostly based on species and points, having the right rig and basic skills to catch a few dabs is essential.

This dab rig is also versatile and will catch a host of other species, such as whiting, pouting, poor cod, flounders, dogfish and gurnards, to name just a few.

How It Works

The boom, although being secured between sliding stop knots or rig stops, is best fished for dabs when positioned tight behind the lead weight. This ensures that the baits are tight on the bottom and keeps them moving across the sand in a natural manner, which is where the dabs expect to find their food.

Being able to turn freely on the rig body means that, even when descending through the water column, there's minimal chance of the trace tangling, especially as the trace is kept deliberately short. It also minimises the chance of tangles if you choose to use a light lead to occasionally bounce the tackle further downtide with the tide flow.

Why Specifically A Wire Boom?

The wire boom doesn't flex as it drops through the water column, helping to reduce the chance of the trace tangling. Also, the extra weight of a wire boom helps the baits to stay on the sea bed – when the line between the weight and the rod tip is allowed to fish just slack. In fact, competition anglers using this type of boom will often fill the triangular hole created where the 'T' shape meets the actual boom with a flattened lead. You can also add lead wire, or clip on large split shot to the end of the boom behind the swivel, to increase its weight further to nail the bait to the bottom. This tactic dramatically increases dab catches.

Fewer Tangles

Using a fluorocarbon hook-trace line instead of clear mono also reduces the chances of tangling, as the fluorocarbon is slightly stiffer in character and tangles less when swirled about in the tide. Plus it offers greater abrasion resistance when you're catching large numbers of fish on the same rig.

Luminous Bead

Another little tip is that, when fishing in deep water, slightly coloured water or low-light conditions, by adding a single

Build Sequence

01 Begin with 18 inches of 40lb clear mono and, to one end, tie on a size 4 rolling swivel.

02 Slide on a rubber rig stop or a short section of neoprene tubing to act as a stop knot.

03 Now slide on a 5mm bead, followed by the boom and another 5mm bead. Now slide on another neoprene-tubing rig stop or rubber rig stop.

04 To the free end of line tie on a size 2 French snap link to take the lead weight.

05 To form the hook trace, take 30 inches of 15lb to 20lb fluorocarbon and tie one end to the boom swivel.

06 Form a 12in loop in the free end of the hooklength. Tie in a double granny knot to secure the 15in loop.

07 Create a short 6in hooklength by cutting one side of the loop six inches below the granny knot. This also gives you a second lower hooklength about 18 inches long.

08 To both hooklengths tie on a size 2 to 4 Kamasan B940 Aberdeen hook.

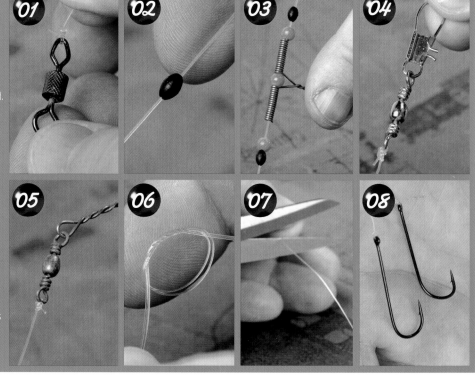

3mm luminous green bead directly behind the hook you can double or even triple your catch of dabs. Add just the one bead, because two have proved less effective in trials.

Other Species

To use the rig for other free-swimming species such as pout, whiting and gurnards, slide the boom up the rig body about six inches. You'll still catch occasional dabs, but will also increase the catch rate of the other resident species.

Hook Size

Keep the hook size to no more than a size 2. This is plenty strong enough to land even the odd ray that might take one of these small baits, but the smaller hook sizes and baits will also further increase your bag of smaller fish generally.

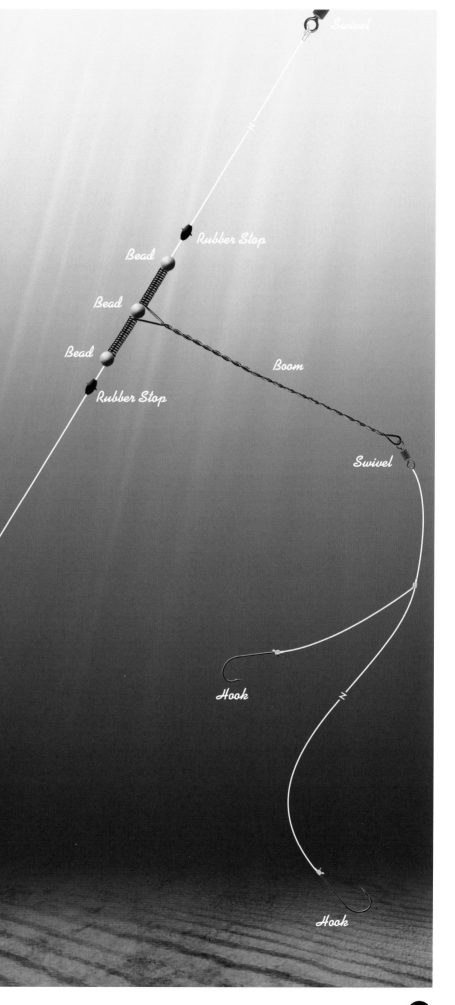

Swivel

Rubber Stop

Bead

Bead

Bead

Boom

Rubber Stop

Swivel

Hook

Swivel

Snap Link

Hook

Lead

Catch More

Learn how to target plaice by following this definitive guide full of top tips and tricks…

BOAT PLAICE

The plaice is fairly distinctive but, on occasions, can be confused with the dab and the flounder. To be sure you have a plaice, there's a simple way to tell them apart: the plaice has a series of four to seven bony knobs running rearwards from the eyes towards the pectoral fin on its upper side, whereas these are absent on both the flounder and the dab. The confusion arises mainly from the fact that the plaice has vivid spots, usually pale to bright orange, but the flounder can also occasionally show faint spots on the back, so be aware that this is not a reliable method of visual identification.

The plaice's colouring is usually light to mid-brown with the vivid orange spots, but occasionally it can be greyish when living over gravel and shingle. The belly is pearl white, sometimes with dark blotches.

Female plaice become sexually mature at three to seven years old and males at two to six years old. The spawning season runs from January to March. This occurs offshore in water of more than 30 metres deep. The eggs are carried in the surface layers and take 10 to 20 days to hatch. Over the next four to six weeks the larvae and post larvae remain in the surface column and it's at this time that, in conjunction with other body changes, the plaice's left eye migrates to the right-hand side of its body, and as this change occurs the plaice becomes a true flatfish and measures three-quarters of an inch in length. →

Plaice are sporting, great fun to catch and excellent to eat!

Boat Record
10lb 3oz 8dm – H Gardiner, Longa Sound, Scotland, 1974

Boat Specimen Target Weight
5lb

The plaice can live to be 30 years old and is somewhat territorial, moving little once it's established on a certain patch of ground. It's not known exactly how large the species can grow, but years ago a plaice of more than 22lb was trawled up. Just imagine if they were left alone to grow – that's food for thought!

The plaice eats a varied diet, including brittle stars, worms, crabs and shellfish such as razorfish and mussels. It's also adept at nipping the siphons off sand clams that are poking out of the sand. The plaice is a formidable predator and will eat sandeels, and specimens have also been found with sprats and gobies inside their stomachs.

When And Where To Fish

The plaice inhabits waters all around the UK and Irish coast, but is also found northwards throughout Norwegian waters to the Russian border, all around Iceland and off the southern tip of Greenland. It also inhabits the western coast of Europe as far south as the Mediterranean.

The UK and Irish season is typically from mid to late February when the plaice return inshore after spawning, right through to November, but they're in prime condition from June onwards. The biggest plaice tend to show in August and September although, generally speaking, smaller plaice can be caught all year round.

The plaice favours offshore sandbanks and can be found resting on the inclines of them, typically at the base and in the middle of the rise, but occasionally on the top of the bank. It prefers sand, or a mixture of sand and shingle, but will also live over fine shingle and shell grit, and also seed mussel beds. The most famous sandbanks for plaice are The Skerries off Dartmouth and The Shambles off Weymouth, both marks that produce large numbers of big plaice.

Plaice can be caught on all sizes of tides, but often offshore the smaller neap tides produce the better fishing because the drift of the boat will be slower and the presentation of the bait to the fish better, with the fish being able to catch up with the bait more easily and pounce on it as it passes by.

Dinghy anglers should also look at the mouths of smaller estuaries where plaice often sit on the sandbanks leading into the main channels. The species also favours mussel beds and bigger examples offshore also tend to lay up on cleaner sand surrounded by rocks, and such marks will often produce specimen-sized fish. The edges of reefs that feed onto clean sand are also good places to try.

Plaice Tackle

It pays to fish light for plaice because the bites can sometimes be delicate, plus

The plaice has bony lumps running from the eyes to the pectoral fin on its upper side.

How To Build A Plaice Sliding Leger Drift Rig

There are many varied rigs for plaice, but keeping it simple is the best approach. A simple sliding leger rig is often the most effective.

01 Onto the leader, slide on a Zip slider boom, followed by a 5mm bead.

02 To the end of the leader, tie on a size 4 rolling swivel, and to the other end of the swivel tie on four to six feet of 12lb to 20lb fluorocarbon.

03 Slide on five or six coloured beads. A good combination is green and black, along with yellow and red.

04 To finish, tie on a size 1 Kamasan Aberdeen B940 hook.

Rig Tip

Although clear monofilament is okay to use as a hook trace, experienced plaice anglers prefer fluorocarbon. This is not just because it is more difficult for the fish to see, but more because it has a slightly stiffer nature than mono and is more resistant to abrasion when drifted over shingle and broken shells.

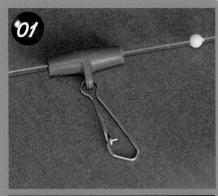

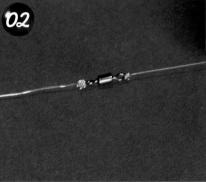

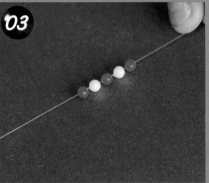

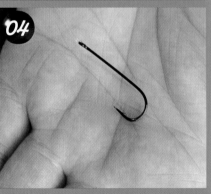

Rig Tip

light tackle maximises the fun with the smaller fish.

A 6lb to 12lb-class rod matched to a small multiplier, such as the ABU 5500C or the Abu Revo Toro 50, loaded with 10lb braid and a 12lb fluorocarbon leader, make a great combo. Some anglers prefer a light 8ft spinning rod, such as an ABU Soron, plus a Shimano or Daiwa 4000-sized fixed-spool reel, again loaded with light braid. This type of outfit maximises bite detection.

How To Hook Plaice

A plaice will show on the rod tip initially as a series of short rattles. When this occurs, be prepared to release up to 20 feet of free line from the reel. This will keep the bait on the sea bed and allow the fish time to fully take the bait and hook into its mouth. After a few seconds, flip the reel into gear and simply allow the line to come tight to set the hook. There is no need to strike!

Baits

The plaice typically likes a combination of baits. A good one is to thread on a blow lug, or a 4in section of black lug. Now thread on a whole king rag about five to six inches long and leave about two inches of the rag's tail free to wriggle to add movement. Finish with a long, 5in sliver of squid cut thinly to provide more movement. A thin sliver of white mackerel belly can also work well.

Other baits to try are mussels, razorfish, clams, white rag and maddies, again as combination baits. Queen cockles also make great bait for big plaice.

Top Tip
Alternate green and black beads on the hook trace can be deadly – especially when fishing over pea-mussel beds.

Rag is always a firm favourite for plaice.

Small reels coupled with 6lb to 12lb-class tackle will provide you with the best sport.

Five Top Tips

Keep It Tight!

When drifting over the banks, on some days it's important to keep the bait as tight to the sea bed as possible. If bites are few and far between, shorten the hook trace to just 12 inches. This means that the movement of the bait will be reduced and will keep the bait bouncing on the sand. Longer traces can see the bait fluttering too far up off the sea bed to attract the plaice.

Heavy Weight

A good skipper will set the boat up to drift on alternate sides each drift to give all the anglers equal fishing opportunity. If you're fishing under the boat and cannot let much line off for fear of tangling with the lines of the anglers on the other side of the boat, use a heaver weight than is actually required to ensure that the bait is on the sea bed and fishing correctly. Also lift the lead up off the sea bed occasionally to make the bait more visual to nearby plaice.

Watch Leads

Flat, watch-type leads are good choices. Being flat, they sit tight to the sand and keep the bait presented close to the sea bed, but they will also 'puff up' spurts of sand as they cover the ground, which can also attract the plaice in towards the baits. Some of the flat, pear-shaped carp leads are also excellent for the same reason.

Spooning

Sometimes, adding a flashing spoon above the hook can be of benefit. These can be smaller spoons no longer than half an inch, or bigger metal spoons of up to two inches. Tie these to the main hook trace, then below the spoon tie on nine inches of 12lb to 20lb fluorocarbon, then a series of coloured beads and the hook. A spoon is best used when the tide is running hard to make the spoon twist, flutter and flash.

Drilled Bullet

If you need the bait to be hard on the sea bed, in between the plastic attractor beads, add a small ¼oz to ½oz drilled bullet. This will guarantee that the bait is kept dragging across the sand where the plaice take most of their food.

Spreader-Bar RIG

These rigs are becoming popular again with plaice anglers.

History

Spreader-bar rigs were first mentioned in sea angling books in the late 1800s and were then made of brass wire. These were used mainly for flatfish and general bottom feeders. They disappeared off the scene after the Second World War, but were successfully resurrected in the 1980s by Brian and Duncan Swinbanks of KF Tackle, based in Tobermory in the west of Scotland – and again proved highly effective for many species of fish.

Over the past few years anglers in southern England, west Wales and Ireland have again gone back to a spreader-bar system with much improved results over conventional boat rigs, especially when targeting gurnards, haddock, whiting and flatfish.

Whereas in the past spreader bars have been made with the lead weight attaching to the middle of the spreader bar via a fixed clip link, the modern version sees the spreader bar moulded into the lead weight. This current version was the 'hot' boat rig during the summer and autumn of 2009.

How It Works

The spreader bar does several things that a conventional rig does not.

Firstly, when drift fishing and trotting the spreader-bar rig well away from the boat and as the line angle decreases, the lead weight and bar scuffing along the sand creates disturbance in the form of little rising clouds of sand that nearby fish will see and move in to investigate.

Over mixed broken ground, when the spreader bar comes in contact with rocks and boulders, the metallic 'clang' again alerts the fish, especially gurnards, codling, ling and haddock, that are particularly drawn in by rhythmic noise.

There's also a theory that the spreader bar vibrates the

water as it's dragged along; that fish pick this up through their lateral line, and again move towards the source in the hope of food.

On days when the boat is steady at anchor, and not swinging with the wind and tide, dropping a spreader bar onto rough ground can be especially effective for a variety of fish, especially wrasse, pout, cod, ling and strap congers.

The spreader bar is wide enough to sit across gaps in the stones and boulders and prevents the lead weight from snagging, so tackle losses are reduced and bait presentation is improved. It also means that the baits will be sitting down between the

Build Sequence

01 You can buy fixed-lead spreader bars from good tackle shops, but for those of you making your own weights either an 8oz or 10oz bomb mould is needed. Drilling a hole about an inch down from the top to take stiffish coat-hanger wire or a heavy gauge of stainless-steel wire achieves the same result.

The wire needs to be about 20 inches long with the lead weight positioned dead centre.

02 Using pliers, make neat, round eyes in the ends of the wire to attach a hook trace. To each eye add a size 6 swivel via a clip link.

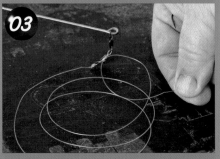

03 To each spreader-bar eye swivel, tie on 15 to 30 inches of 20lb to 25lb fluorocarbon line to form the hook trace.

04 Onto each hook trace slide on alternate coloured attractor beads. Blue and red or orange and yellow beads are good choices, and in between add a plastic attractor spoon – red, gold or silver being good colours to use.

05 Finish the traces by adding size 2 to 1/0 hooks – Kamasan B940 Aberdeen hooks or equivalent patterns are ideal.

06 Attach the spreader bar to your leader or main line via a clip-link swivel to reduce the chance of any twisting as the tackle descends and when retrieved.

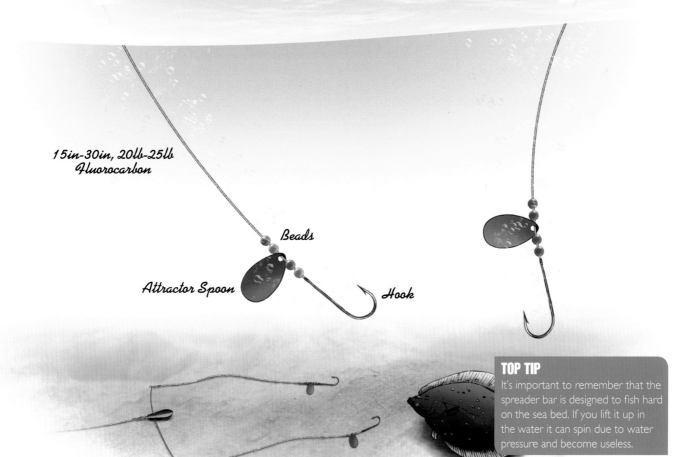

Snap-Link Swivel

Coat-Hanger Wire
Or Heavy-Gauge Wire

8oz to 10oz Lead

rocks, where the rock-dwelling fish expect to find food.

The rig's biggest advantage is that it presents baits spread well apart and rarely tangles. You can use hook traces up to 30 inches with no problem, or you can stagger the lengths of the traces, offering a choice by fishing one at 30 inches and the other at 15 inches. The beauty is that the baits are kept hard on the sea bed and always inside the typical feeding zone

of gurnards, flatties, haddock, ling and cod.

With two hooks available you can also offer two different baits and using, say, mackerel strip on one and rag on the other will show whether different species are taking just a particular bait.

Blue and red, black and red or orange and yellow beads were the killing colours last year, but it pays to experiment. In deep water, switch to

alternate red and luminous yellow beads; these really work for haddock, whiting and codling. For flatfish mix red and white. Black and green also seem to be working well of late for plaice, in several parts of the UK and Ireland.

Adding a small plastic or metal attractor spoon in between the beads increases attraction and vibration, but both work really well, especially over clean sand for flatties and gurnards.

15in-30in, 20lb-25lb
Fluorocarbon

Beads

Attractor Spoon

Hook

Total Sea FISHING

Total Sea Fishing provides sea anglers with the all the hottest news and gossip, along with expert advice from the best anglers in the business. You'll find no-holds barred reviews on all the latest tackle, detailed step-by-step features on how to catch the fish you seek, plus several pages dedicated to your catch reports.

Grab yourself a great subscription deal at:

dhpsubs.co.uk/totalseafishing

Summer
BREAM
On The Ledge

Roger Mortimore hops aboard *Wight Sapphire* to do battle with some hard-fighting black bream on the Christchurch Ledge, off the Dorset coast.

A couple of gentle taps turn into a bite that completely slams my rod tip over. Line is being ripped from the spool at an almighty rate as a hard-fighting fish dives for cover. I steel myself for the scrap ahead, my grip on the rod increases, muscles straining to hang on to the frenzy on the end of my line as beads of sweat run into my eyes. Slowly but surely, aided by the rod's action, I bring it under control. My wrist aches as I gain enough line to see a huge shape appear from the depths. "Look at the size of this," shouts skipper Bob Gawn as he slides the net under a huge black bream. Once on board it slams the scales down to 4lb 4oz and smashes my personal best! I have a huge smile on my face and I am so pumped with adrenaline that my hands are trembling and my legs are shaking.→

Black Bream Facts

- The British boat record for black breams is a fish of 6lb 14oz 4dr caught by J A Garlick from a wreck off the South Devon coast. It has stood since 1977.
- The shore record is a massive 6lb 8oz 6dr taken in Creux Harbour, Sark, by R Guille in 2001.
- Black bream spawn in the spring between April and June. They mature as females when they reach 20 centimetres and may change sex to male at 30 centimetres. All bream over 40 centimetres are male.
- They lay their eggs in nests and the male stays at the nest to guard the eggs until they hatch.
- Male bream display a brilliant blue on their head and fins during spawning.
- Bream prefer rocky or rough ground and wrecks, feeding on small invertebrates, crustaceans, algae and small fish.
- Although black bream can be caught at night, daytime is usually best.
- Black bream are common along the south coast, around the West Country and parts of the Welsh coast.

Black bream are pretty fish, great fighters and good to eat.

I first met Bob Gawn while visiting The Helm, a well-known hostelry in Westport, Co Mayo, during the 2008 Westport Skate Festival. Bob is the skipper of *Wight Sapphire*, based at Yarmouth on the Isle of Wight. When Bob suggested that I join the boat on a trip out for black bream in the spring I jumped at the opportunity. I caught my first bream off Dartmouth, way back in the early 1970s. I was amazed at how hard these little fish fight all the way to the boat.

A date was selected just after Easter, when the tides were right and, hopefully, the weather would be settled for our outing.

After driving south through fog, I arrive at our pick-up point in Lymington in brilliant sunshine and no wind – perfect conditions.

After parking by the pontoon I meet fellow anglers Sean Nally, who has driven over from Hythe in Kent, and Matt Towgood from Southampton. Lymington is a regular pick-up point for Bob and handy for mainland-based anglers. Once all of our gear is loaded aboard we meet the other anglers, Owen Giles, Becki Florence and Phil Smith. As we set sail the captain points the bow of the boat toward the Christchurch Ledge.

We rig up ready for action as we travel along; some of the

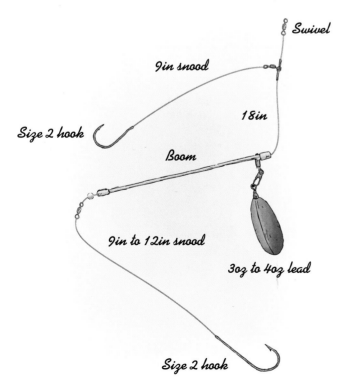

Swivel

9in snood

18in

Size 2 hook

Boom

9in to 12in snood

3oz to 4oz lead

Size 2 hook

guys choose to use a single-hook running leger while the others opt for a one-up-one-down rig, as bream often feed a few feet off the sea bed. Bream have small mouths, so small hooks are the order of the day. Our rigs are armed with size 4 and size 2 hooks baited with tiny strips of squid. Sean has a box of party squid – the little ones that are just a couple of inches long – and these are cut down the middle to make long, thin baits as they outfish a normal strip of squid by miles.

I rig-up with a Fladen Super Sensor II rod; it's a little like a spinning rod that has soft fibreglass push-in tips. This will give me excellent bite indication and allow me to enjoy the fight of these feisty little fish. I match the rod with a Shimano Stradic3000 fixed-spool reel loaded with 15lb braid topped with 20 feet of fluorocarbon leader.

After a short steam we arrive at our mark and Bob drops anchor in the deep water just off the edge of the ledge. With more than 30 years of experience, Bob knows that the first shoals of bream tend to stay in the deeper water for a couple of weeks before they move up into the shallower water on top of the ledge. The flood tide we are fishing is a little disappointing with just nuisance dogfish and pout but, suddenly, Sean is into a better fish that turns out to be a lively smoothhound that's taken his squid bait. A few minutes later and Sean is

into another fish that's putting up a good scrap, but it's not a bream-type scrap and as it nears the surface we can see that it's a bass of around 2lb. We now have four species aboard, but where are the bream?

Bob explains they can be a little slow on the flood tide and that the ebb is usually more productive. We were about to find out how correct his advice was…

Slack water only produces a few more dogs, then skipper Bob shows the way by landing the first bream, a lively little female of around 1lb 8oz. I score next with a male fish around the same size as Bob's; the males are pretty fish with striking blue tinges on the head and fins. As the current picks up, so does the fishing and soon we are all having bites, but they are finicky and difficult to hit. The crew soon come to grips with hitting them, though, and Owen's spinning rod takes on a satisfying curve as he hooks his first bream of the session.→

Hectic action saw three bream come aboard at the same time for Phil Smith, Bob Gawn and Roger.

Top Tips

01 Black bream have small mouths so use hooks in sizes 6, 4 or 2 and match your bait size to the hook you're using. The top baits are small strips of squid, mackerel or sandeel and tiny pieces of peeler crab. A tiny squid mounted on a size 2 Aberdeen is perfect.

02 Despite their small mouths, black bream have some good strong teeth so use snoods of 15lb or 20lb breaking strain to avoid being bitten off.

03 Use light gear where possible to gain the best sport possible from these great little fighters.

04 Bream can be finicky feeders giving very gentle bites, using a tiny bait on a very sharp size 6 hook will help convert bites to fish landed.

05 If you still miss the bites, try using braid; its lack of stretch will hit those sneaky bites better.

06 When the current dies down bream may feed up off the sea bed, so try using sandeel feathers with size 6 or 8 hooks baited with tiny pieces of squid or mackerel.

07 Bream spawn in the spring, so try to return most of your fish so they have chance to reproduce.

Phil, Becki, Bob and I all hit into these hungry bream, but poor Matt had been missing bites until his rod suddenly bends double. This looks like a much better fish, and so it proves to be; it's a cracking personal-best bream for Matt at 3lb 9oz.

Everyone is buzzing now and catching regularly, the ebb is in full flow and has really put the bream on the feed, exactly as Bob predicted. All the small fish are returned to grow bigger with just a few of the better sized examples kept for a fish supper. I must have been into double figures in catch numbers when I spotted another bite. As I pick the rod up I feel another couple of taps then it just slams over and line peels off the spool. This is a much better fish and it's putting up a hell of a scrap; even at the back of the boat I have trouble lifting its head up so that Bob can net it. Eventually it's safely in, my trembling hands remove the hook and it's a new personal best for me. I have to sit down and compose myself, my hands are shaking so much that I can't bait up again for a while.

Unfortunately, the 60 tiny squid in Sean's box soon run out as his squid soon became 'our' squid, so we decide to call it a day and head for home. Perfect conditions and great banter on a glorious spring day and we've all caught plenty of fish. Isn't this what it's all about? Isn't this the feeling that we all go fishing for?

Roger's over the moon with his new PB 4lb 4oz bream.

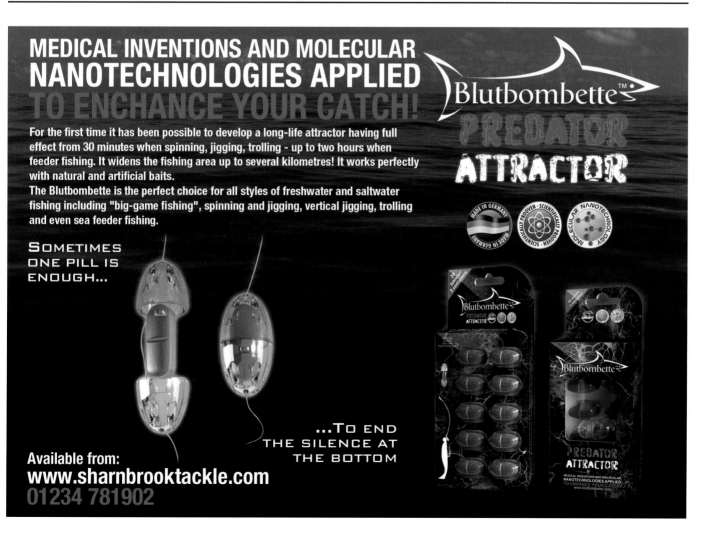

Black Bream RIG

This easily adjustable rig is great for chasing bream as they change depth.

History

It's impossible to say where or when this rig was invented. But, it was probably used in a more archaic form as far back as the end of the 19th century, when anglers using brass booms fashioned a similar rig.

What we do know is that it became popular with anglers targeting black bream on the ultra shallow Cardigan Bay reefs during the early 1970s. This was when boat anglers realised that trout spinning rods and small fixed-spool reels loaded with just 8lb line maximised the fight with these small, but sporting fish.

It was the change to plastic booms, such as the Avis Boom, and lightweight rigs that saw the current rig come in to being. It's become the most consistent rig when targeting single reef and wreck bream and also proves effective with reef trigger fish.

How It Works

Some anglers make this rig without the beads to trap the boom between. This is a mistake when using the neoprene stop knots, as you want the boom to rotate freely around the rig body line to increase natural bait presentation. The beads are more efficient when in contact with the boom and allow free rotation.

Adjustable

The reason this rig incorporates sliding stop knots and uses a relatively long rig body length is that it can be adjusted in an instant to adapt to where the fish will be in the water column while the tidal flow changes. The total length of the rig body and the extended trace should not be longer than the rod, to allow easy netting of the fish at the surface.

During slack water the bream rise up off the reef or rocky ground and work a few feet up off the bottom. When this is the case, slide the snood up the rig body to fish just below the top connector swivel. When the tide starts to run strongly and the bream drop back down to the sea bed, slide the boom down to just a few inches up above the lead. This constant adjustment of the depth at which the bait fishes will dramatically increase your catch rate during the day.

Snood Length

Although 36 inches of hooklength is a good all-round length for general fishing, don't be afraid in fast running water to increase this to six feet to give more natural movement to the bait in the current. Similarly, in slow or near static tidal flow reduce the length,

Build Sequence

01 Begin with at least 40 inches of 30lb clear mono. Tie on a Gemini Lead Clip to one end.

02 Slide on a 5mm length of neoprene tubing, pass the line through the tubing, back over on itself and back through the tubing the same way. Now pull the line tight to lock on the tubing. This forms a sliding stop.

03 Slide on a 3mm rig bead, an Avis Boom or similar boom and another rig bead. Slide on another 5mm section of neoprene tubing, then tighten the line to form a second sliding stop.

04 To the free end of 30lb mono tie on a size 6 rolling swivel.

05 The hook trace is 36 inches of 15 to 20lb fluorocarbon line or clear mono tied to the end of the boom. Finish the hooklength by tying on a size 6 Kamasan B940 Aberdeen or Sakuma equivalent.

How To Form A Neoprene Stop Knot

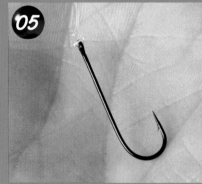

if necessary, to just a couple of feet. The latter also works well if the bream are shy and coming short, giving just a few hardly discernible pecks on the bait.

Shy...

Bream can sometimes be suspicious of a bright red or yellow boom, if the water is very shallow and gin clear, even when they're in a big and hungry shoal! In this case and if there is enough tide run, increase the hook trace to fully flow it out. If the water is clear, but has little tide run, then change to a clear-coloured boom. Occasionally over reef ground, when fishing tight to the sea bed, a black boom will improve the catch rate, as it blends with the reef better – or you can colour a boom black using a permanent marker.

Hard Wearing And Invisible Line

Experienced anglers prefer to use fluorocarbon for their hooklengths rather than mono. As is often stated, fluorocarbon is more resilient with a harder surface than mono and is less sensitive to abrasion from the reef and from the teeth of the bream.

This counts for triggerfish, too, when you are constantly landing good numbers of fish. Also, it's less easily seen by the fish in clear, shallow water than mono.

The teeth abrasion factor is also another reason why long-shanked Aberdeen pattern hooks are the best choice. These give the bream and triggerfish, which are often found among the bream during high summer over reef ground, something to chew on before they get to the hooklength line.

'Weight' For It!

One last tip to get the best from this rig is to use a lead weight only just light enough to stay in contact with the sea bed. By occasionally lifting the rod tip and releasing a couple of feet of line, you can bounce a bait downtide to find the fish. Trotting bait back when fishing among other anglers can enable you to find the bigger fish, which often sit downtide, right at the back of the main shoal.

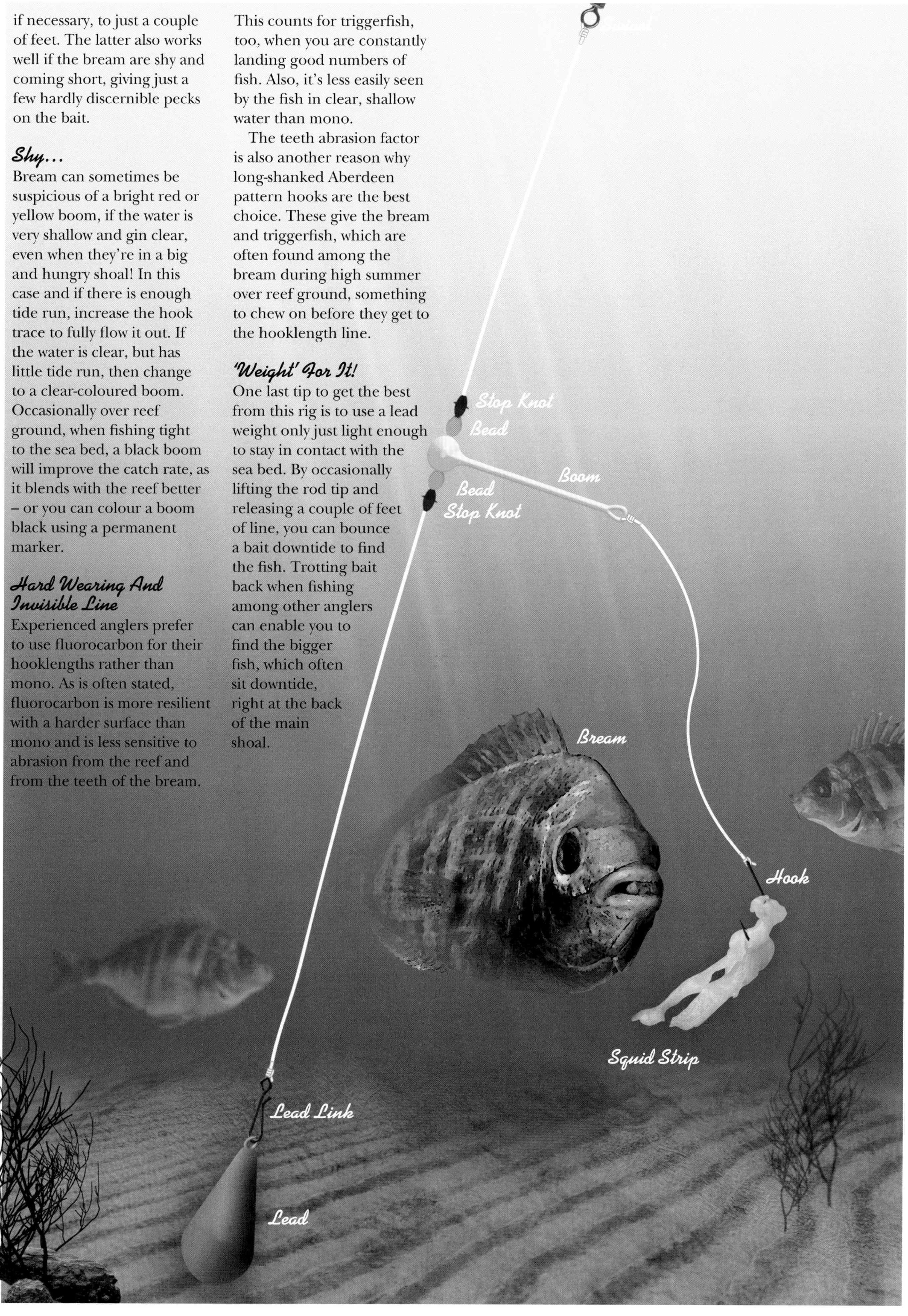

Swivel

Stop Knot
Bead

Bead
Stop Knot

Boom

Bream

Hook

Squid Strip

Lead Link

Lead

Catch More LING

Ling are popular with boat anglers because they're great sport and very tasty. We show you how to specifically target them.

Ling belong to the cod family and but are difficult to confuse with adult cod fish due to their distinct shape. The upper jaw is slightly longer than the lower and both are filled with needle-sharp teeth. The body is longer and slimmer than the typical cod family, with the lateral line arching upwards over the pectoral fin. The second dorsal and anal fins extend almost to the tail, the tail being rounded in shape with the fin edges often white. There are also distinct dark blotches at the back of both dorsal fins.

Body coloration can differ, with ling found over cleaner ground having mottled-brown backs with silvery-white bellies. The fish over rough ground take on a more olive-green coloration on their backs, fading to mottled brown on the flanks with white bellies.

The spawning season falls between March and June and occurs in water over 200 metres in depth. Ling favour specific spawning areas in the North Sea, Icelandic Sea and off the west coast of Scotland. Each female lays 60,000,000 eggs and hatched fish reach eight inches in size within the first year.

Their habitat is typically rough ground that's adjacent to high-rising rock pinnacles and heavy wreck structures in depths up to 400 metres or more. They will also hunt through broken ground, deliberately flushing prey out.

Their diet is mainly small whiting, codling, pout, poor cod, flatfish and smaller members of their own kind→

Tackle

For reef fishing look at a true 20lb-class boat rod; a length of 7ft 8in to 8ft is about right. Look for a supple tip – because ling can bite gently when drift fishing – but with progressive power in the mid-section. Use a stiff butt to give lifting power.

Penn GTI reels or Shimano TLDs holding 300 yards of 20lb line are fine for reef work, although for fishing 20lb braid the more expensive Penn TRQ 100 is the top reel because it offers a narrow profile but has tough, high-speed gears for working in deeper water.

For general wreck fishing in deep water, 30lb-class tackle is a better choice. Braided line works better than mono because you need less lead to stay in contact with the sea bed. Longer rods over eight feet with braid guides are also best married to the Penn TRQ 100 reel, or the Daiwa Saltist in an equivalent size. Alternatively, try Shimano's TLDs or a 7000-sized Abu.

How To Make A Mackerel Flapper Bait For Ling

01 Place a whole mackerel on the bait board and chop the tail off at the root.

02 Cut upwards from the tail root carefully following the backbone, but only cut as far as the pectoral fin; leave the fillet attached to the head.

03 Do exactly the same on the reverse side.

04 Slide the freed fillets to one side, now cut through the backbone just behind the head and remove it.

05 This leaves the head intact and the fillets free to flap in the water to add movement as the bait drifts over the sea bed.

06 Pass the hook through both jaws at the front, leaving the hook point well clear of the bait for maximum hooking ability.

When And Where To Fish

Ling are found all around the UK, being resident on the English Channel wrecks, the North Sea wrecks and over rough ground right along the west coast of Britain, especially Scotland. They also feature heavily right around the Irish coast, especially on the wrecks off Cork and Kerry, and up the west and north coast where rough ground predominates. They're also common off Iceland and along the coast of Norway.

They can be caught throughout the full 12-month period, but the best of the fishing is over inshore rough ground through the late summer and autumn periods – this is generally for smaller ling to 25lb.

The bigger fish are found on the deeper water wrecks, which produce the best in the winter period, especially either side of Christmas until late March, with the January to March spell typically producing the bigger fish.

Ling over rough ground tend to be concentrated in the heaviest and roughest areas, in among the boulders and working in tight to rock pinnacles and vertical ledges. They feed best with some tide run, when the smaller fish are closer to the sea bed and where the swimming is easier.

Wreck ling also like some tide running but tend to feed most in the hours either side of the middle tide period when the run is less strong.→

Ling Rig

01 Take 24 inches of 50lb/60lb mono.

02 Tie a strong 2/0 rolling swivel to one end.

03 Slide on a 5mm bead then a hollow plastic boom about 10 inches long.

04 Slide on another bead and tie on another size 2/0 rolling swivel.

05 To the lower swivel, using a four-turn uni-knot, tie on five foot of 150lb clear mono.

06 Slide on a luminous-yellow muppet; one about six inches long is ideal.

07 The hook needs to be an 8/0 for rough-ground fishing, and a 10/0 when wreck fishing. Partridge Sea Beast hooks are good as they are strong and have ultra-sharp points.

Note

The luminous muppet is important. The fish follow the scent but also home in on the luminescence as they approach the bait. It's proven that the yellow muppet will dramatically improve your catch rate.
This rig works both on the drift over rough ground and when drifting over wrecks. It also works well static legered when fishing at anchor over rough ground.

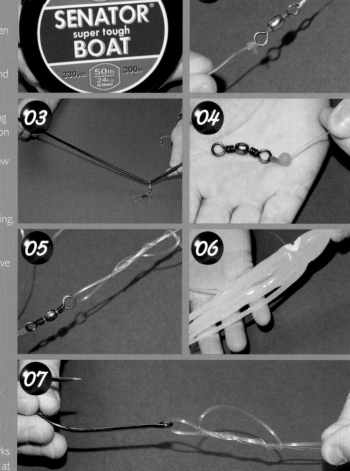

01 When drift fishing you can change your muppet for a large rotating spoon. Ling love the light flash of a chrome spoon, plus the spoon gives off vibration that the ling respond to even in very deep water.

02 When fishing at anchor for ling, it often pays to simply lift the bait up in the water a few feet then drop the bait back again periodically. This often triggers a quick bite because the fish respond to vibration and the visual aspect of the bait as it flutters down in the water.

03 Ling bites, on a slower drift, tend to be savage attacks – the ling literally grabs at the bait and turns away. When drifting at speed, ling have less time and may only get the opportunity to nip at the end of the flappers without eating the whole bait – you get the bite but miss the fish. To avoid this, as soon as the bite is felt, release a few feet of line to give the ling time to grab and take in the bait.

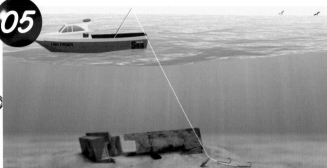

05 Take note of the time lapse from when the skipper says it's okay to drop the gear at the start of the drift and when the first fish or bite occurs. This is important. If the first part of the drift is long, then you'll already have released a lot of line to maintain contact with the sea bed. It's far better to wait until you're more certain that the exact, fish concentrated, area is approaching and drop your gear just before you get there. This means that your line is more vertical, your tackle less likely to snag, plus your bite detection is improved.

06 Another way to fish for ling is to use a two-hook rig made from 100lb mono with blood loops tied in two feet up and five feet up from the lead link. Cut the blood loop to produce a short, 10in hook snood, add a muppet and tie on a size 8/0 hook. Bait the hooks and simply bounce the lead weight on the sea bed to give the ling some noise to home in on.

TOP TIPS

07 You can make muppets more effective by leaving them in bright sunlight, or, better still, use a camera flashgun to give them increased illumination. The muppet is allowed to slide over the mackerel bait when fishing.

08 Take your time with ling when playing them up through the water column. Ling are particularly subject to suffering blown swim bladders due to the change in water pressure. But experienced anglers play ling slowly and carefully, allowing them to semi-adjust to the water-pressure change and, in moderately deep water, they will make a recovery and go back to the sea bed on many occasions – though not always. You can also pop the swim bladder with a hook point to release the pressure and allow the fish to swim back down. If they don't go down, you can always pick up on the way to the next drift and keep them for the table, but it's best to give them the benefit of the doubt!

09 Always have three different baits already prepared to limit the amount of time it takes to rebait after a caught fish, missed bite or lost tackle. This often allows you two separate drops on the same drift, instead of one, which will, again, increase your catch rate.

04 When both rough-ground and wreck fishing you can reduce tackle and fish losses by using a weak link between the lead link, on the boom and the lead weight. Use either a wire tie lightly twisted onto the lead weight for easy release, or simply a length of weak 15lb line about three inches long.

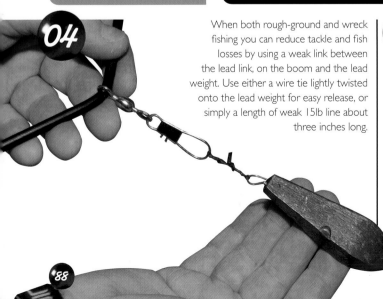

10 Other baits that produce good ling are whole large squid or double squid baits, fresh herring, whole whiting and pouting or fillets from larger pout and whiting. Ling like fresh baits and have excellent scent-hunting abilities, so have no problem finding any non-oily-fleshed fish on the sea bed.

TANDEM RIG

A consistent catcher of pollack, cod and ling with lures, bait or both!

History

The original rig was called the 'killer gear' on the basis that it was able to catch two fish at once when worked over reefs and wrecks situated off the southwest of England. It also accounted for numbers of large winter cod and ling from the late 1960s onwards. Nowadays the word 'killer' has been dropped and its new name is the 'tandem boat rig'.

The idea behind it is that it simulates small shoal fish by using plastic muppets, artificial eels and soft-plastic and rubber shads. By using a heavy weight, you can punch through the shoals of pollack above the wreck to reach the bigger cod, pollack and ling below. It can also be used with larger 8/0 or 10/0 hooks instead of the lures, and baited with fillets or whole flapper mackerel to target large bottom feeders.

The rig fell out of favour for a while over the past decade, with anglers tending to fish single lures for maximum sport, but has now made a real comeback due to the increased numbers of cod available offshore over the past few seasons.

How It Works

The rig is best fished on 30lb-class tackle capable of landing two large fish at once.

Fishing this rig is easy! Using a heavy weight to punch through the smaller fish, allow the rig to touch bottom, then retrieve just two or three feet of line, then lift and lower the rod tip in a slow and methodical lift of the main arm to work the lures in an up-and-down sequence. This simulates small fish swimming in the water column.

A Pirk For The Job

A good tip is to change the weight for a chrome-coloured pirk. This will have the weight to power through the upper column of shoal fish, but will present a big, fluttering target when worked that will add vibration and attraction and, by itself, is capable of taking big fish. You can also add another muppet to the hook on the pirk for more movement and attraction.

Build Sequence

01 Begin with 60 inches of 80lb to 100lb line and tie on a size 3/0 Mustad oval split ring at one end. When targeting ling use 100lb clear mono to help combat the ling's sharp teeth.

02 About 20 inches up from the split ring, tie in a blood loop, making sure that the finished loop is at least five inches long.

Around 36 inches above this, tie in another blood loop. This wide distance between the top and bottom loop is deliberate. When a big fish takes the top lure and another is hooked on the lower lure, it allows the big fish to be netted on the surface at the side of the boat, while the other fish is still well down in the water and less likely to break free or tear the hook-hold out.

03 Finish the main rig by tying on a strong size 1/0 rolling swivel.

04 Cut the blood loops close to the knot on one side only to create a single 10in-long hook snood.

05 When using muppets, slide the muppet onto the line, then slide on a 5mm bead and tie on an O'Shaughnessy-type hook size 4/0 to 8/0 to suit the lure size.

When using artificial eels or jellyworms, just slide the eel or worm over the hook and onto the shank, with the hook left well clear. Good hooks are Mustad 79515s in sizes 4/0 to 6/0.

To present shads, again just slide the hook through the body and bring it out of the back of the shad facing upwards. Again, the proven Mustad 79515 hook is ideal for most shads in sizes 3/0 to 6/0.

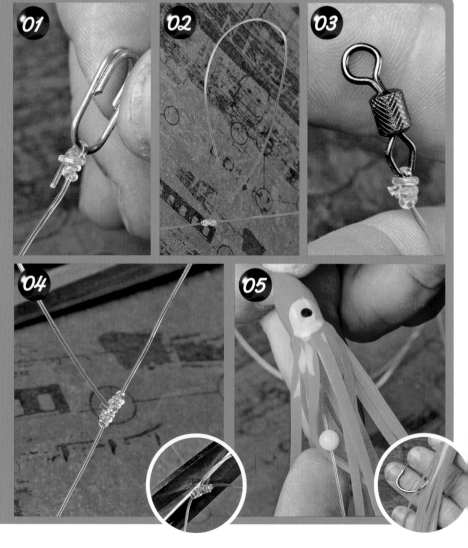

Best Colours

The colours you choose for the muppets can be critical to what you catch. Cod favour pink muppets, ling seem to take luminous yellow, with pollack being suckers for black. Of course, all colours work, but these named colours do tend to pick up a higher percentage of these individual fish. Also try mixing two colours on the same rig.

Eels

As for artificial eels, such as Red Gills, Eddystones and Powerworms, then a black body with either a red tail or yellow tail will work well, or an all red or white body. Sidewinders are great lures too, especially the rhubarb-and-custard colour.

Shads

The same applies to shads. The top fish takers are black, red, clear blue and white. Anything with sparkle in it also works. The Berkley Ripple shads are really hot lures because they have ripples formed in the sides that add much more vibration and these also take a lot of fish in all sizes.

Alternatives...

Remember, though, you can ignore the lures and choose to fish just two baited hooks, or add a long strip of mackerel to the hooks used on the muppets. This little dodge often increases the catching power of this rig on days when bites are difficult to come by. It's also ideal for drifting over scattered wreckage over more open ground, by just keeping the lead in touch with the sea bed to fish the baits dragging tight to the bottom. This is often how the biggest ling and cod are caught.

To limit tackle losses you can also tie a few inches of lighter line to the oval split ring. This should be about 20lb and will break off should the lead weight become snagged, freeing your rig and any attached fish!

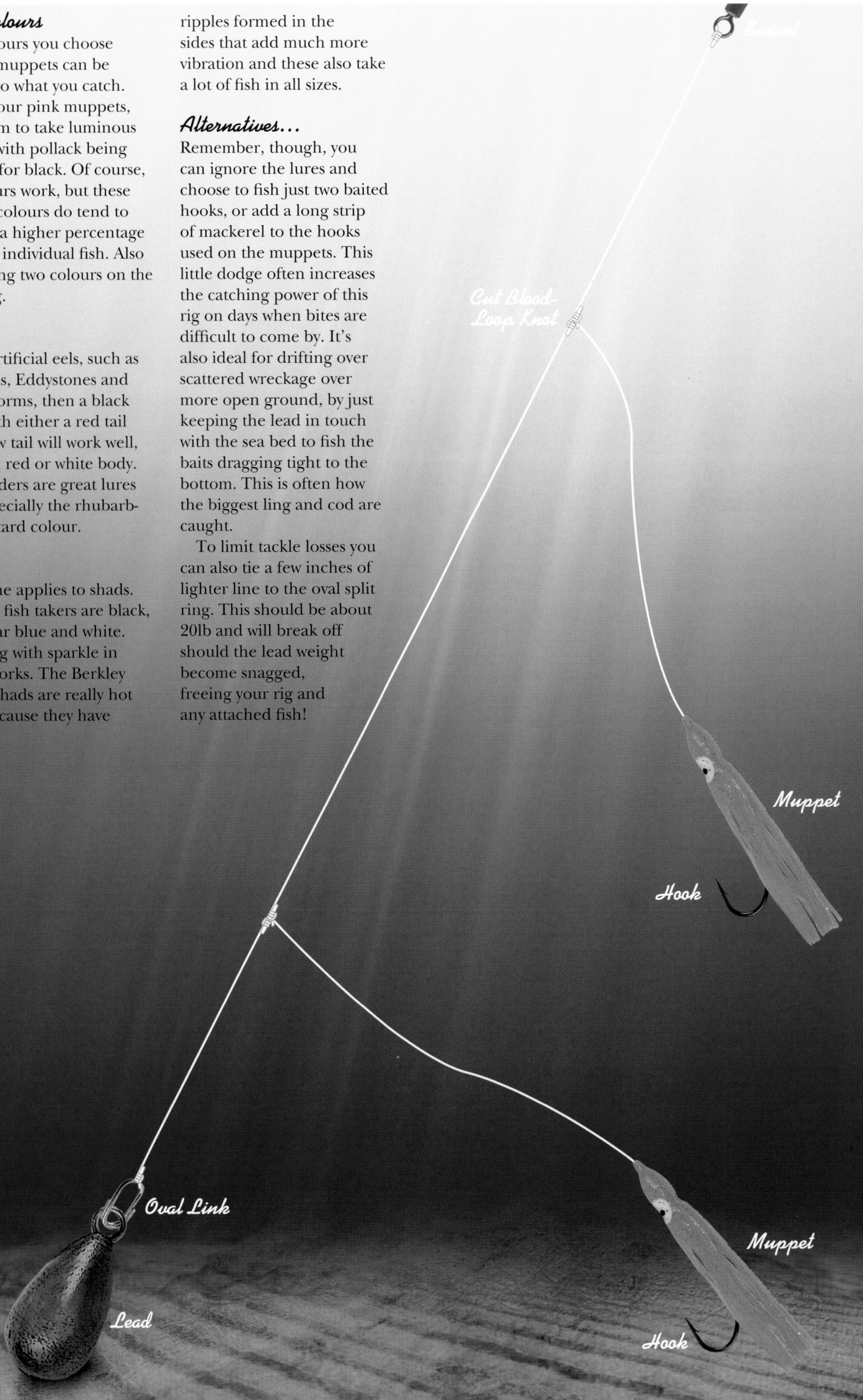

Swivel

Cut Blood-Loop Knot

Muppet

Hook

Oval Link

Muppet

Lead

Hook

Catch Your Best-Ever BOAT COD

Follow our top tips and tricks to give you the very best chance of bagging a massive cod on your next boat trip!

A big cod is the crowning glory for most boat anglers.

Boat Record
58lb 6oz – Noel Cook, off Whitby, North Yorkshire, 1992

Boat Specimen Target Weight
20lb

Although the British best is the 58lb 6oz cod, it is worth taking note of the 103lb cod caught back in May by German angler Michael Eisele. The facts of this capture are relevant to our specimen quest. The cod was caught in 90 feet of water at the end of a poor day's fishing some 10 miles off the island of Soroya, Norway. What's significant, as will become clear shortly, is the depth in which it was taken and that the fish appeared to be a loner. It was also caught an hour before low water when the tide run was easing.

In the UK it will be the offshore wrecks that are most likely to produce a 20lb-plus cod. Working clockwise, however, do not discount the inshore rough ground off the northeast coast, which does give up a few fish of this size. The most obvious would be the long-distance wrecks lying some 20 miles plus out in the North Sea off Whitby. These wrecks have a long history of big cod.

Equally good would be the wrecks in the English Channel with those off Ramsgate, Dover, Eastbourne and Brighton being very good bets, along with the wrecks off Lymington, Weymouth and Plymouth.

The Bristol Channel, on both the English and Welsh sides, is another hot area, but this will normally be over reef and coral ground relatively close inshore in shallowish water. There are wrecks here, too, but it's the inshore ground that gets fished the most.

The wrecks in the Irish Sea are very little fished, but have given up cod to specimen size in the past. You cannot discount these and the opportunity is there for big fish. Wreck trips from Aberdovey, Pwllheli, Caernarvon, Holyhead and Amlwch can put you on wrecks holding big cod.

The Mersey Estuary used to produce this size of fish from the C22 buoy and other marks in years gone by. The cod are still there, but big cod are fewer in number here nowadays, although the chance remains.

The next good area would be the wrecks that are little accessed from the west coast of Scotland and those off Orkney.→

These hold big cod, but lack the angling pressure to prove how good they could be. The other obvious prolific area would be around the Faroe Islands!

Around Ireland, possibilities exist off Wicklow, again on the Irish Sea wrecks, the wrecks off the Waterford and Cork coast, off Kerry, west of Clare Island in Mayo and on the wrecks off Donegal, especially Culdaff.

Seasons

The Whitby wrecks tend to be fished between May and September, with the inshore rough ground then favoured from September through to March. In the English Channel the wrecks can see cod to specimen size present from late May through to late March, although the prime period is from January to March.

In the Bristol Channel records tell us that the bigger fish show in late November, with the December to mid-February period the best.

The cod are available in the May to March time period in the Irish Sea, but most trips are made in the summer when the weather allows, although winter fishing could well prove the best. It's the distance of the wrecks that restricts the fishing in winter as well as the weather here though.

The Mersey fishes best between December and

On a big cod, believe it or not, the head alone accounts for nearly a third of the fish's weight!

February. The west of Scotland is likely also to be dictated by the availability of winter boats and weather, with the summer months from June to September seeing the bulk of fishing done.

Ground Feature

Big cod will work rough ground inshore picking up poor cod, pouting, herring, whiting and other smaller species. They favour ground that is ideally of a varying depth where they can work through big boulders, lifting reef edges, rising rock pinnacles and rock ledges. These bigger fish hug the sea bed where the bulk of the food is. Depth ranges from 60 to 150 feet or more, generally speaking.

If there are rising rock pinnacles, then expect the cod to be working around the base of the pinnacles only. They rarely lift much more than 20 feet up from the base.

It is the same on the shallower reef ground inside the Bristol Channel. Here the fish work the reefs and coral ground targeting whiting and pouting. Depth can be anything from 40 to 80 feet or more with the cod working tight to the sea bed at all times. Shallow water of less than 100 feet in depth can and does produce big cod! The exception to this is if there are sprat shoals in the water column. If sprats are resident, then the cod are likely to be preoccupied and less likely to take baits or lures.

But what of the wrecks? These can be inshore wrecks in just 80 feet of water, but tend to be in deeper water roughly between 150 and 250 feet. In the Irish Sea, some of the wrecks are in 300 feet plus with a fast tide run. Invariably all wrecks are surrounded by patches of rough ground that

Use a rod with suitable power to work the chosen lures and size of target fish. A 20lb to 30lb-class outfit will cover most bases.

Use smaller reels, such as this Abu Revo Toro NaCl 60, to enjoy greater sport!

Build Sequence

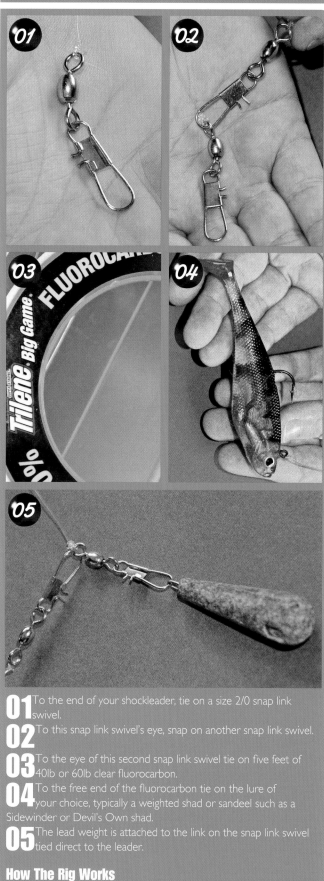

01 To the end of your shockleader, tie on a size 2/0 snap link swivel.

02 To this snap link swivel's eye, snap on another snap link swivel.

03 To the eye of this second snap link swivel tie on five feet of 40lb or 60lb clear fluorocarbon.

04 To the free end of the fluorocarbon tie on the lure of your choice, typically a weighted shad or sandeel such as a Sidewinder or Devil's Own shad.

05 The lead weight is attached to the link on the snap link swivel tied direct to the leader.

How The Rig Works

This is worked by letting the lead weight touch bottom, then retrieving about 10 feet of line back onto the reel. Now you just lift the weight up and down using your wrist and forearm to literally bounce the lure in an up-and-down action just up off the bottom. This is deadly for big cod!

---

the tide working around the wreck has scoured out, or, more typically, surrounded by sandbanks.

Remember that the smaller food fish that the cod prey on use the reef ground, and especially the wrecks, for protection – so the cod will be right in among the reef or wreck structure.

Tides

On typical shallow to mid-depth reefs, the cod tend to like the bigger tides because these disturb more food for them to prey on. In areas where the tide is very fast, then the smaller neap tides may be the only option to fish because at other times the tide run will see the boat drift too quickly. The alternative on reef ground in less than 100 feet of water is to anchor and uptide cast big baits and let the cod follow the bait scent trail.

On the offshore wrecks invariably it is the smaller neap tides with less tide speed that are best. These allow the boat to drift over the wreck more slowly, extending the time that

the baits or lures are in the killing zone. Ideal conditions are wind against tide, which will slow the speed of the boat right down. In areas where the natural tide run is lessened, then the bigger spring tides can also produce good catches, but drifting faster than one and a half knots makes life very difficult even when using braid lines to minimise the effect.

Cod on the reefs will feed as the tide is running hard, and bites ease away as the tide reaches slack water and gets ready to change direction. But on the wrecks the best period for big cod to feed often falls on the late ebb as tide flow eases and just after slack water as the new flood tide picks up speed. As the tide flow increases, the cod fall back into the shelter of the wreck.

Weather Conditions

In the deeper water over reefs and wrecks, some daylight does penetrate, so flat-calm seas and bright sunshine tend to fish less consistently than, say, a cloudy day with →

a light breeze to ruffle the sea's surface and limit light penetration would. The less light reaching the depths, generally the better the fishing will be. Rougher seas often fish well over rough ground and on the shallower wrecks because it adds a little colour to the sea.

In areas such as the Bristol Channel and the Mersey, then the water is pretty much always carrying heavy colour, so the fish feed even in broad daylight. That said, take notice and you will see that cloudy days and reducing light levels towards dusk often coincide with improved fishing.

In all areas west-based winds are favoured, with east wind fishing way less consistently.

Tackle

On the reef ground when anchored, then for downtide fishing off the stern of the boat, go for a 20lb to 30lb-class rod matched to a reel holding about 300 yards of 30lb braid or 200 yards of 30lb mono. Good reel examples are the Penn Fathom 20 or the Shimano TLD20, or the Penn TRQ30. This tackle is also good for basic wreck fishing.

When anchored and uptide casting, a 9ft 6in to 10ft uptiding rod casting 8oz and a big bait is perfect. Reels suitable for this are the Penn 525 Mag 2 loaded with 20lb mono and a 50lb shockleader, or the ABU 7500i Elite loaded with 25lb line and a leader. Akios, Shimano and Daiwa also do similar reels.

When working lures for wreck and rough-ground cod, then anglers prefer a lighter approach. A popular choice is a 20lb/30lb rod about eight feet in length with a soft tip, but with power quickly coming into the upper mid-section and feeding into a stiff butt. Smaller 15-size reels are good with this size of rod, such as the Penn Fathom 15 or TRQ15 loaded with mono backing and 300 yards of 20lb to 30lb braid. Add a short 12ft shockleader of 30lb fluorocarbon to the braid. Some anglers fish lighter with a 12lb/20lb rod and a low-profile reel, such as the new saltwater ABU Revo Toro NaCl 60 with just 20lb braid and a short leader.

Baits And Lures

Big cod will take fresh baits such as whole mackerel

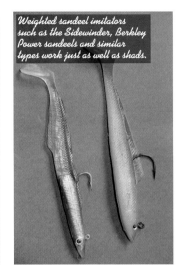

A giant jighead is a cracking lure and easy to work. It's simply a heavy jighead, to which you attach any unweighted shad you fancy on the day!

Weighted sandeel imitators such as the Sidewinder, Berkley Power sandeels and similar types work just as well as shads.

flappers, herring flappers and large pouting flappers worked on long traces and boom rigs over and into wreckage when wreck fishing.

When uptide fishing over reefs, big lug and rag baits work very well. Make these worm baits a good 10 inches long and tip them with a strip of squid to add movement. Alternative baits are whole squid, or half-body sections of bluey.

There are so many lures that take cod, it is hard to choose which work the best and it will inevitably be a personal choice born from experience.

However, go for weighted shads in 4in to 6in sizes in black, red, yellow, white and clear. Good ones are Berkley Ripple shads, the Shakespeare Devil's Own type, Sidewinders, Eddystone eels, Delalande shads and Savage lures but most work well.

Pirks are now classed as somewhat old fashioned, but they still produce big fish and remain popular in the northeast of England. Those with a bend in their design tend to flutter down when on the drop, which is when the cod often take them.

Five Top Tips

Lead The Way

When drift fishing, constantly change your lead weight to ensure that your line is working as vertically as possible in relation to the rod tip. If the line is streaming away at a shallow angle and with the weight constantly being released to keep in contact with the sea bed, then this is when you will lose most tackle. A vertical lead and lure a few feet up off the sea bed is both working efficiently and well away from most snags.

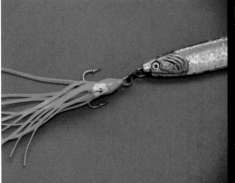

Get Jiggy With It!

For really big cod, try an 8in to 12in rubber shad or worm mounted on a heavier 8oz-plus leadhead. This can be lowered straight to the bottom and again either jigged up and down just off the bottom, or retrieved for the first 20 feet then dropped back and the pattern repeated.

Fluorocarbon

Use fluorocarbon up to 50lb for your hooklengths when uptide fishing and working fresh baits on long traces in front of booms, or 40lb to 60lb fluorocarbon when working lures. The fluorocarbon is far more resistant to the teeth of cod and also when coming into contact with reef stones, barnacles or sharp wreck structure and loses you fewer fish than mono will.

Muppet!

The effectiveness of pirks can be improved by adding a pink muppet to the treble hook. Pink is the killer colour for cod over wrecks. In more coloured water, change to a luminous-yellow muppet.

Added Attraction...

When working big flapper or fillet baits, try adding a large pink or luminous muppet over the nose of the bait to both add colour and more movement via the legs of the muppet. You can also add fillet baits to the hooks on pirks too!

Two-Boom ATTRACTOR RIG

This is the boat version of a popular shore rig – it's great fished on the drift.

History

Although a boat fishing rig, the two-boom system has been adapted from the shore rig that incorporates two booms and is designed to spread the baits apart but also to limit tangles, making this rig ideal for fast dropping through the water column to maximise fishing time.

This rig, however, unlike the shore rig that's fished against a static lead, is designed to be used on the drift to cover as much ground as possible. It also features attractors designed to visually 'advertise' the baits to fish that are lying outside the scent trail of the baits, making it highly effective for a large number of bottom-feeding species.

The rig came into use, in various forms, about 20 years ago.

How It Works

Having the two booms spread apart allows you to fish baits both hard on and just up off the sea bed. With the top one slightly higher in the water column, it targets fish swimming and feeding up off the sea bed such as whiting, haddock, coalfish, codling, pollack, pouting and will also take small ling. The lower hook trace takes the flatfish.

This is also why we incorporate the adjustable crimps. If you just compress these enough to hold the boom and beads in place, but with finger pressure move the crimp up and down (holding the neoprene tubing in place too), then you can easily move the booms to new positions. For instance, if you are fishing the booms one near the top swivel and the other roughly in the middle of the rig, and all the fish are coming to the middle boom, then slide the middle boom down to be just above the lead link and slide the top boom down to the middle. You now have two baits in the feeding zone and can double your catch. It works in reverse, too, if the majority of the fish are taking the top-boom bait.

The rig is best fished with luminous beads. It was originally designed for deep-water drift fishing and the use of luminous beads helps highlight the bait in deep, dark water. The silver spoon, which proves highly effective in clear water, suggests that light levels at depth are enough to give reflection that will attract fish, though vibration from the spoon is also important.

However, the red spoon is also effective, especially for species such as gurnards and haddock.

The spoon is mounted below the first small bead, because we want it to have some ability to revolve. If you mount it with the larger number of beads above it, the weight of these pressing against the spoon via water pressure stops it revolving. This is an important point.

The fluorocarbon hooklengths are also important because fluoro is a little stiffer than mono, and will not tangle as easily – plus it has a higher abrasion resistance when in contact with the sea bed, and also from the needle-like teeth of whiting, small ling and other bottom-feeding fish.

Keep the hooklengths no longer than 12 inches to

Build Sequence

01 Begin with 46 inches of 60lb clear mono and, at one end, tie on a SALT lead link.

02 Slide on a Sakuma adjustable crimp, a 3mm rig bead, a SALT shore boom, another 3mm bead and another adjustable crimp.

03 Above these, slide on another adjustable crimp, a 3mm bead, a SALT shore boom, a 3mm bead and another crimp.

04 Finish the main rig by tying on a size 4 rolling swivel.

05 The hook traces are 10 inches of 20lb/25lb fluorocarbon. To each hook trace slide on a 3mm luminous bead, a silver or red plastic attractor spoon and three luminous 5mm beads.

06 Finish each hook trace by tying on a size 2 Kamasan B940 short-shank Aberdeen hook.

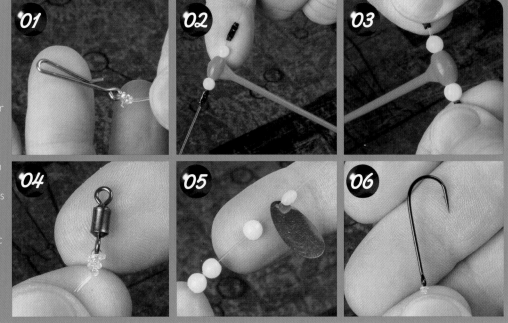

minimise tangles. It is best to use a stiffish longer boom like the SALT boom, or similar, because this helps keep the bait away from the main rig line.

Some anglers make the mistake of fishing this rig vertically with a heavy lead, although it will catch like this. It is much more effective, however, when used with leads just light enough to keep in contact with the sea bed and letting plenty of line out to fish the rig at a shallow angle. This presents the baits both naturally and at slightly different heights to offer different presentations to appeal to as many types of fish as possible.

If you want to add more illumination to the rig, fish it with a luminous lead weight. This is especially popular in Ireland and can increase the catch rate in deep water.

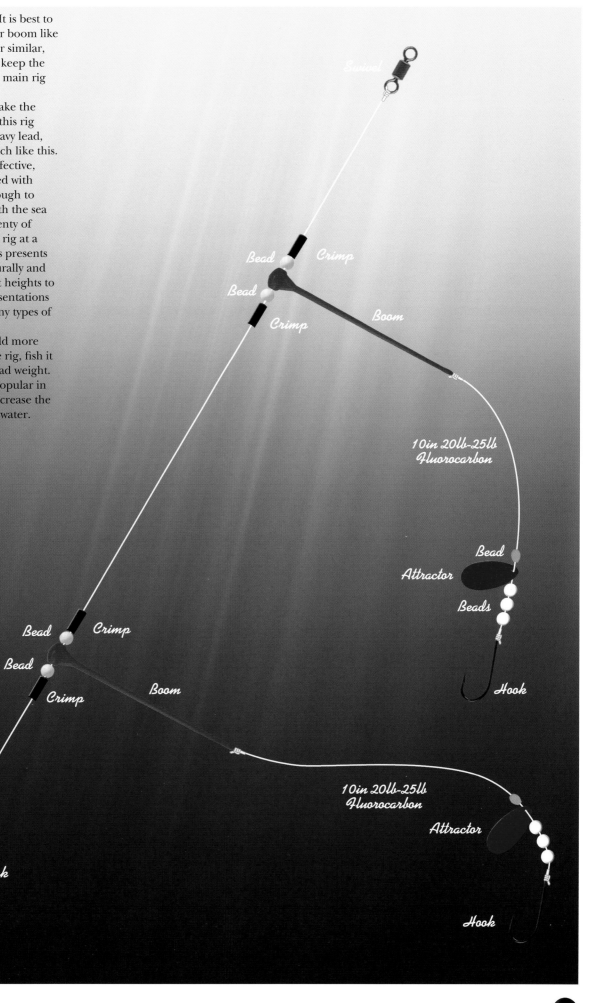

Swivel

Bead   Crimp

Bead

Crimp   Boom

10in 20lb-25lb Fluorocarbon

Bead

Attractor

Beads

Hook

Bead   Crimp

Bead

Crimp   Boom

10in 20lb-25lb Fluorocarbon

Attractor

Lead Link

Hook

MOLE RIG

This rig seeks out fish among the cracks and hidey-holes of rough ground.

History

This rig came from the basic 'two-hook drift rig', which has proved so successful throughout the UK and Ireland since the mid-1970s.

A similar rig incorporating short hook snoods was being used in Northern Ireland during the late 1970s over marks such as The Maidens off the port of Bangor, targeting mainly wrasse and cod. But, at the time, the rig, though used by a few UK anglers, was not universally adopted over here.

This particular rig was christened the 'Weymouth rig' after it starting winning boat matches along the south coast a few years back, and it's since done well for both competition and freelance boat anglers across the UK. The name has since changed in some quarters to become the 'mole rig'.

It's called the 'mole' because the rig works very tight to, and in among, the sea-bed rocks searching out all the nooks, cracks and hidey holes, and has proved very effective for wrasse, as well as pout, whiting, codling and small ling that are normally best targeted with longer, flowing traces.

The rig also works well with whiting and dabs over clean sand, plus gurnards.

Build Sequence

01 Begin with a short, 24in section of clear 60lb mono. Tie a size 4 rolling swivel to one end.

02 Thread the free end through a 12in hollow plastic boom and tie on a size 4 three-way swivel by one end eye.

03 At the other end eye of the three-way swivel, tie on another short, 14in section of 60lb clear mono line and add another three-way swivel by one end eye.

04 Add an 18in section of 30lb fluorocarbon line to the other end eye of the swivel.

05 The middle eyes of the three-way swivels take a second and third hook snood. Again, this needs to be 30lb fluorocarbon, and keep this short at no more than six inches.

06 On both the snoods tied to the middle swivel eyes, slide on a bright luminous green bead followed by a luminous yellow bead, another green bead and finish with a second yellow bead.

07 The hooks need to be quality Aberdeen patterns such as Kamasan B940s in size 1/0.

08 The leading 18in hook snood has the same bead combination added but, in between the last two beads closest to the hook, add in a 1in red-plastic revolving spoon. Finish with another size 1/0 Aberdeen.

09 It's important to keep to the basic dimensions and keep the overall length of the full traces to no more than 36 inches. This rig works best kept short!

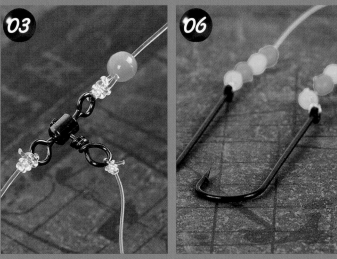

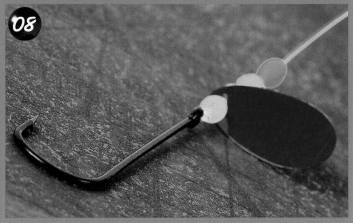

How It Works

It's designed to be fished while on the drift, although the rig can be effective at anchor in a decent tide. The high visual impact of the beads on the individual hook traces being so close together is designed to achieve a big target area that, even in deep water, will draw fish to the baits. It also has the advantage of the spoon, which will flutter and rotate as the rig moves; this adds movement and vibration to the rig. By putting three baits very close together this will maximise scent and give fish the incentive to chase the baits down if the boat is moving at speed in the tide.

You can see now that the choice of the luminous beads is critical. It's these that add the visual impact, the luminescence drawing the fish to the baits. This is especially apparent in very deep water, but also in shallower water that still carries a little colour after a storm, or where tidal currents lift sediment up off the sea bed to muddy the water a little.

The fluorocarbon for the hook traces is also important. This is chosen for its stiffness to avoid tangles and to maintain proper presentation of the baits on the drift.

It also pays to add a short weak link of line between the hook and the weight clip on the boom, or, easier still, to add a stiff-wired paper clip that will pull straight should the hook become snagged, saving both tackle and fish.

The biggest mistake you can make with this rig is to be scared of losing it. It's at its most effective literally kept in very tight – and in almost constant contact with the bottom. If the rig is not banging hard ground, then it will be less effective. The wrasse are down in the rock cracks and behind bigger boulders and stones, and will only chase baits that literally work past their noses. This is why the rig fishes best with braid, as the contact with the ground is maximised and lets you work the rig as close to the sea bed as possible. Braid will also magnify the bites better.

Some anglers have trouble hitting bites with this rig. The knack is not to strike at the fish at the first bite but risk the gear, allowing just a few feet of line off the reel to leave the rig momentarily static on the sea bed for a couple of seconds. Then simply let the line come tight to feel the fish. There is no real reason to strike. With the boat on the drift the tightening line will pull the hook home. Often instantly striking only sees you lift the bait away from the fish and the bite is lost. Done properly this gives a good 75 per cent return on the bites you have.

Just as in all fishing, if you have consistent bites, but fail to hook the fish, instantly drop down in hook size. The wrasse will often take the 1/0s, but the smaller pout and other bottom dwellers find them too big. Going down to a size 2 Aberdeen will still see wrasse caught in numbers, but will also add the smaller species to your bag.

Rolling Size 4 Swivel

Boom

Lead

24in 60lb Mono

6in 30lb Fluorocarbon

Bead

Four Alternate Luminous Yellow And Green Beads

Size 1/0 Hook

Size 4 Three-Way Swivel

14in 60lb Clear Mono

Size 4 Three-Way Swivel

18in 30lb Fluorocarbon

6in 30lb Fluorocarbon

Four Alternate Luminous Yellow And Green Beads

Size 1/0 Hook

Four Alternate Luminous Yellow And Green Beads

Size 1/0 Hook

Attractor

A BRILL Day

Mike Thrussell heads to Weymouth to see if he can up his species count to 103 by adding a brill to this remarkable list.

Some may find it unbelievable but after more than 50 years of sea fishing there's one species that has always eluded me – brill. I've been on several boats where this lovely flatfish has been caught, yet my baits only seemed to appeal to plaice and turbot.

So, the time had come for me to make a determined effort to break my brill duck. I pored through books and reports to gauge the main ports where brill were commonly caught and, although several existed, it seemed to me that Weymouth offered some real consistency with the Shambles Bank the noted hotspot.

I duly organised a day aboard Colin Penny's famous charter boat, *Flamer IV* – a vessel that's renown for anglers bagging good numbers of brill to specimen size.

Hardly A Shambles!

As we approached the Shambles Bank, the wind was coming in from the southwest, and tidal action breaking white and downtide of the bank edge was clearly visible. There were white caps on many of the waves further off, too, and the wind was increasing.

Colin set up the drift to run us first towards the bank, then up its incline and down the other side.

The first drift was fairly uneventful, but on the second a couple of turbot →

Top Tip

Make sure you trim off any tag ends on knots. These are the most likely cause of tangles should the hook trace hang up on one of these when the bait is being dropped at speed to the sea bed. If these are clipped close it's highly unlikely that any tangles will occur and you can fish with confidence.

Mike Thrussell (r) holds up his first brill after a 50-year drought.

Know Your Quarry

To give me the best chance of catching one, I decided to learn as much about them as possible. Brill are left-sided flatties – both eyes are on the left – and are longer and more oval in shape than turbot, which are more diamond shaped. They are also covered in tiny scales, while turbot have hard tubercles scattered across the skin.

Adult brill are found living on the inclines of sand and shingle banks in depths of 20 to 250 feet, but usually they're found in shallow water.

They are predators and lie buried in sand and fine shingle with just their eyes showing – waiting for prey such as sandeels, small whiting, codling, poor cod, pouting and even other small flatfish venturing by. Then, with a flick of its tail to launch it forwards, it opens its mouth and sucks in its prey.

This little bit of fact told me that it's important to have the bait hard on the sea bed, occasionally lifting it up to make it more tempting. The most likely place for a hit is when the boat is drifting over the top of a bank and the baits are still climbing up the leading incline – or well past the bank when the bait is sliding down the opposite slope.

The British record for boat-caught brill is one of the oldest and was set in 1950. The fish weighed bang on 16lb but brill half the size are considered to be specimens. For this trip, however, my mission was to catch my first one, immaterial of size.

were caught, then Barney Wright brought the opening brill of the session aboard.

My heart fluttered mildly when my rod bent into a fish, only for it to be a fat and prime turbot of 4lb… a cracking fish, but not what I was seeking!

Into My Stride

Over the next few drifts a couple of brill were taken, both off the stern section; I was on the starboard side. I was just getting into a rhythm when Colin was forced to move and target plaice, due to the flow of tide, before we could resume our quest for brill and turbot.

While fishing for plaice, I ran back through my research on brill and also tried to remember what the fish already caught were taken on, just to see if I could glean anything that might help – but I couldn't!

A New Plan...

Thinking things over I figured that I'd use a heavier lead weight, 12oz instead of 10oz, to ensure my bait was hard on the sea bed – but I'd also modify my rig. I stayed with the sliding leger but dropped down to 30lb fluorocarbon and increased the length of the hook trace to seven feet. This would provide extra movement in the bait, which would hopefully appeal to the ever-vigilant brill.

Mackerel fillets cut in half lengthways are perfect bait for brill.

Bait

I also researched baits for Weymouth and – although brill will take launce sandeel, long strips of squid or long strips of bluey – the killer bait is a thin strip of mackerel cut full length, ideally from the white belly. This should be no more than one and a half inches wide at the thick end, tapering to nothing at the tail end of the fillet.

This is hooked only in the root of the tail to give maximum movement. You can also add a strip of squid for further attraction alongside the mackerel, but most brill are caught just on the mackerel strip.

Mike opens his account with a 4lb turbot.

TopTip

As soon as the skipper starts the engine ready for a new drift and says: "Lines up," get fresh bait on and be ready. Get your bait in the water and fishing as soon as the skipper says: "Lines down." This maximises your fishing time.

Mike's Brill Rig

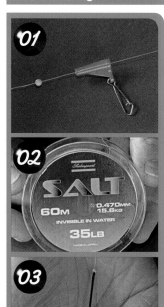

My conversation with skipper Colin confirmed that my initial thoughts on a suitable rig were right. I tackled up with a simple sliding leger and used a 5ft hook trace to minimise tangles.

01 Onto the shockleader, slide a zip slider followed by a 5mm bead.

02 Now tie on a size 4 rolling swivel, and to the free eye of it tie on five feet of 35lb/40lb fluorocarbon.

03 To the free end of the fluorocarbon tie on a size 3/0 Kamasan B940 Aberdeen hook.

Mike draws his fish carefully to the net.

The Shambles Bank

Hungry for more information I checked up on the Shambles. It lies three miles east of Portland Bill and is marked by cardinal buoys at the east and west ends. It's been a nightmare for shipping as scores of vessels have run aground here over the years.

It's formed as a series of undulating sandbanks made up of sand, shale and some shingle. I spoke to someone who sport dives there and he said that the sand dunes make it look like a miniature desert; with sand washing across it, the top of the bank is often barren and mostly made up of fine rippled sand ridges. The bulk of life lives on the inclines of the banks.

The water usually circulates anticlockwise around the bank whose shape is constantly changing due to shifting sands. Even on calm days you can see the tidal edge of standing water that marks the top of the bank. The tide is said to run hardest on the ebb.

In between drifts for plaice, I'd tied up my modified brill rig, plus a spare one in case of tangles to maximise my fishing time.

It was certainly a relief when Colin said we were going back to fish for brill and turbot, and I quickly re-rigged my tackle and cut three long white belly strips of Ammo mackerel. I put two of these to one side so that I had a quick change of bait if needed.

Pressure's On!

The following drifts saw one more brill – a four-pounder – come aboard, but then a certain fear struck me with an announcement I really didn't want to hear. Colin was making just two more drifts before calling it a day.

With time running out the pressure was certainly on for me to see a brill on the end of my line. I've failed in my search for this canny little flatfish so many times before that it was an experience I really didn't want to repeat.

I was fishing under the boat,

so couldn't run much line off, but to give the bait more movement I kept lifting the lead up off the sea bed – about a foot or so.

We were just hitting the rough water line indicating the top of the bank, when I felt a shudder followed by a very distinctive tug on the line. I'd been fishing the reel in free spool and immediately released some line to give the fish a chance of taking the bait properly. I let off about 20 feet of line when I realised I could tangle with the other anglers downtide, so decided to flip the reel into gear and tighten the line.

A dead weight instantly came on→

Barney got in on the act with this lovely 4lb fish.

the rod tip and something kicked hard as it felt the hook. This fish stayed tight to the sea bed and thumped the rod tip a few times. Only when it was forced up off the bottom did it start to kick, trying to dive back down. I knew it was a flattie, but which species?

Nervous

The fish reluctantly came up through the water column, occasionally getting its head down and pumping for the sea bed. My line and gear were still under the boat as I peered into the water. I knew the fish was close, but it wasn't until someone shouted: "He's finally done it!" that I caught sight of the fish I had spent a lifetime trying to coax onto a hook – my first brill!

Colin came to my aid to net the fish and bring my 103rd species over the side and onto the deck. The needle on the scales settled at exactly 3lb – a mighty 13lb off being a record breaker but perfectly formed and, more importantly, the catch made all the effort so worthwhile. Brill… iant!

atch it

A Penny For Them…

Talking at length, Colin Penny said that the banks can fish well on most tides, but on the smaller ones the drift is way slower, potentially resulting in higher catches. On the bigger tides it's necessary to let off line periodically to give any chasing fish the chance to catch up and home in on the bait.

Colin also advised that, although they can be caught throughout the year, the main season for brill is from April to November, with the best fishing being in September and October; the latter being the peak month.

TACKLEH🐾UND.COM

NOW LIVE

One-Up, One-Down
DRIFT RIG

A successful but underused rig, this setup will catch most species!

History

This is a simplified variation on the basic two-hook drift rig that has been in use since the early 1950s, but is designed to present two baits differently when working over clean sand or mixed rough ground, and for targeting a wide variety of species.

Its popularity is due to its ability, with minimal changes, to be used for smaller species, such as plaice, gurnards, codling, whiting and dabs, but it's also an excellent rig for targeting bigger brill, turbot and rays.

How It Works

This rig is designed to fish by releasing a good length of line. This depends on the speed of the drift of the boat and the depth of the water. Typically, a minimum of 50 yards should be released, but release more if need be; up to 100 yards plus is not uncommon if the drift is fast. Aim to maintain constant contact with the sea bed, which can be felt through the braided line on the rod tip as the weight drags across the sea bed.

The more line you let out, the flatter the angle of the rig. Having the bottom bait directly in front of the Zip Slider and weight and the near flat angle of the rig ensures that both baits will be in contact with the sea bed. However, if you want to target both flatfish and species such as codling, gurnards, whiting and others that may be feeding just up off the sea bed, especially when

Build Sequence

01 Begin with 70 inches of 60lb clear mono.

02 At one end tie on a size 4 rolling swivel.

03 Slide on a 5mm bead, a Zip Slider type boom and another bead.

04 About 55 inches above the Zip Slider, tie in a figure-of-eight knot.

05 Now slide on a 5mm bead, A SALT shore boom and another 5mm bead.

06 Just above the last bead, tie in another figure-of-eight knot.

07 Finish the main rig with a size 4 rolling swivel.

08 To the lower swivel add 24 inches of 25lb fluorocarbon and a size 2 Aberdeen-pattern hook.

09 To the end of the boom tie on 10 inches of 25lb fluorocarbon and a size 2 Aberdeen-pattern hook.

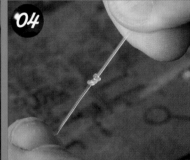

fishing over mixed ground, then release less line to achieve a more vertical angle to the rig and lift that boom-based bait up off the sea bed.

Also continually readjust the size of the lead weight. This should be heavy enough to keep in contact with the sea bed and not occasionally bounce or lift upwards as the speed of the drift increases. Equally, reduce the size of the weight as the drift speed reduces to maximise bite detection.

For inquisitive species like plaice and gurnards you can add coloured beads above the hook if need be. Go for alternate bright and dark colours such as green and black, black and yellow, or red and white.

The choice of boom is important, too. It must be a stiff-plastic type made from a high-density plastic, and not a softer or longer boom that will bend in the tide, because it needs to present the top hook trace well away from the main rig-body line. Also, these tough booms will easily stand landing larger fish, including big rays and turbot.

To adapt this rig for rays, turbot and brill, it's a simple change of hook-trace material and hook. For these species look to use 35lb to 40lb fluorocarbon, and change the hooks to 2/0 to 4/0 Mustad Uptide hooks, or a similar pattern. We recommend that you use fluorocarbon because of its stiffer nature, which minimises any chance of tangling – but equally for its abrasion resistance when in constant contact with the sea bed. Clear mono is okay,

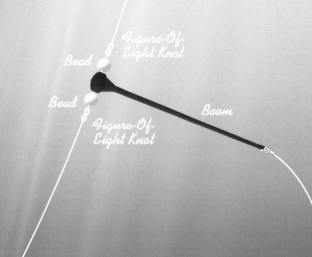

Swivel

Figure-Of-Eight Knot

Bead

Bead

Boom

Figure-Of-Eight Knot

Bead

Lead Slider

Bead

Hook

Swivel

Hook

but does scuff up and needs regular checking, especially when you're constantly landing fish.

Some anglers worry that with the figure-of-eight knot being a strangulation knot it may cause a breakage of the line when playing bigger fish. Given the target species, the knots are under minimal pressure and immensely strong in comparison with direct line pressure. The knots are used because if they were swapped for crimps there is a slight chance of the crimp edge cutting the rig-body line if a big

fish is hooked on that bait. The knots need to be a little way apart and not hold the boom too tightly; it must be free to revolve easily on the rig-body line.

Also, the long gap between the two hook baits ensures that if two large fish are hooked at once, they cannot easily come together and tangle the rig. This is very important!

This is one of the most successful all-round boat rigs and will catch the vast majority of general species anywhere in the country!

Boat Boom
SHRIMP RIG

On the drift or static, this rig is great for sorting out a wide mix of species.

History

No-one seems to know exactly when this rig came into being. Without doubt, though, it was in use off Cork and Killybegs in Ireland back in the early 1990s. But it's one of those rigs that are born from a common thought, and the likelihood is that it was 'invented' simultaneously by many people around the same time.

It remains a little known rig but, as we'll see, it's a relatively simple and highly effective one. It's particularly good for finding all manner of fish when bites are few and far between on those difficult days. In some areas it's called the washing-line rig!

How It Works

This trace is designed to allow the shrimp rig to sweep over the sea bed and cover as much ground as possible. It incorporates a boom, with a normally attached weight on the boom's lead clip to control the long shrimp rig. But the boom is not enough on its own; by attaching a small, ½oz to 1oz ball weight to the more free end of the shrimp rig, the rig becomes controllable and predictable in how it works over the ground.

At Anchor Or On The Drift

The lead weight helps to avoid tangles by keeping the shrimp rig stretched out but, more importantly, being a round ball weight it gives the trace the freedom to roll around, adding movement and covering more ground. With leads on both the boom and the end of the shrimp rig, the rig can be fished when at anchor because it will rarely tangle – but it's also effective when drift fishing, because all five hooks will be dragging on the sea bed where the majority of the fish are feeding.

Bait 'Em Up

The idea is to bait the hooks with tiny slivers of mackerel, squid, rag or lug. With all five hooks baited, this gives a wide scent trail, but also allows the use of different baits to attract different species.

Although this rig can be deadly in clear, even shallow water conditions, it really comes into its own in deep water where light levels are minimal – or in water that still carries some colour after recent turbulence. The luminous glow of the shrimp bodies and the scent from the baits combine to draw fish in – but with the shrimps able to move in the tide, the luminous glow is enhanced due to movement.

Lead Attractor

Some anglers also choose leads that have had a luminous coating applied. This produces a much bigger glowing target area when fishing very deep or semi-coloured water, which again can dramatically increase catches.

Built as described, the rig will catch a wide variety of species such as dabs, whiting, codling, plaice, weevers, pouting, turbot, megrim, dragonets, black bream and a whole host

Build Sequence

01 Start with 30 inches of 60lb clear mono line and, at one end, tie on a size 4 rolling swivel.

02 Slide on a 5mm bead and a 10in hollow-plastic boom followed by a 5mm bead.

03 To the free end of line, tie on a size 4 rolling swivel.

04 Tie one end of the shrimp rig to the lower swivel.

05 To the free end of the shrimp rig, tie on a Gemini lead link. This takes a small lead weight to keep the rig from tangling.

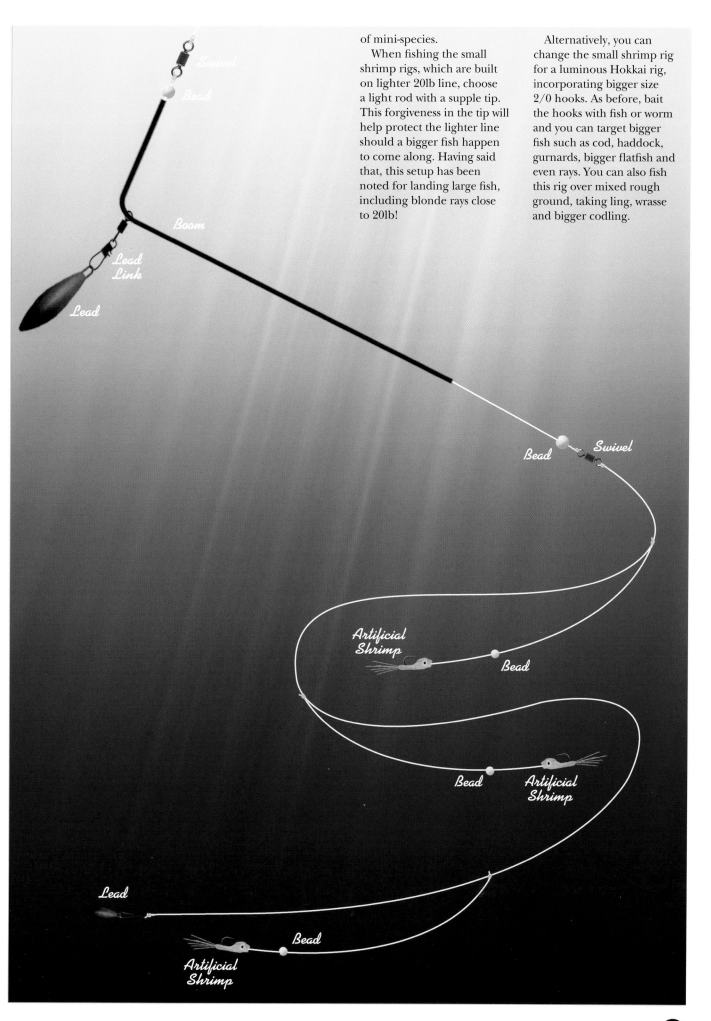

Swivel

Bead

Boom

Lead
Link

Lead

Bead   Swivel

Artificial
Shrimp

Bead

Bead   Artificial
Shrimp

Lead

Bead

Artificial
Shrimp

of mini-species.

When fishing the small shrimp rigs, which are built on lighter 20lb line, choose a light rod with a supple tip. This forgiveness in the tip will help protect the lighter line should a bigger fish happen to come along. Having said that, this setup has been noted for landing large fish, including blonde rays close to 20lb!

Alternatively, you can change the small shrimp rig for a luminous Hokkai rig, incorporating bigger size 2/0 hooks. As before, bait the hooks with fish or worm and you can target bigger fish such as cod, haddock, gurnards, bigger flatfish and even rays. You can also fish this rig over mixed rough ground, taking ling, wrasse and bigger codling.

TOPE RIG

If tope are your target this is THE rig to use, but don't skimp on components.

History

This rig is designed around a basic sliding leger, but encourages early hook-up of the tope to minimise any chance of deep hooking. It is also ultra-strong, plus it presents bait naturally on the sea bed where the tope spend the majority of their time hunting.

It was initially developed in Cardigan Bay, Wales, where much of the tope fishing is done in ultra-shallow water, often just a few feet deep, where the tope will take bait then run fast and far before slowing down to turn and eat it.

This rig is extremely effective and has, without doubt, landed tope well in excess of the current UK record, but the fish have been released alive for conservation purposes.

How It Works

The rig is designed to flow out in the tide and present the bait with some movement, with the long trace allowing the bait to wander freely over the sea bed. More importantly, the length and strength of the long trace gives enough length that, if a big tope should be hooked, any line coming into contact with the tope's body will have the strength to combat any potential abrasion through contact with the tope's rough skin.

Bolt-Rig Principle

Having the zip slider running freely between the two swivels means that the tope can turn, run off a few feet and build up speed before it comes up against the lead's dead weight. As the lead weight lifts up off the sea bed and the line tightens, this has the same effect as a carp angler's 'bolt rig' and self-strikes the tope early on its first run. With a sensibly set drag on the reel, the angler only needs to hold the rod until it comes into its full compression curve for the hook to fully sink home – invariably in the scissors or front jaw of the fish. Deep hooking is minimised due to this 'bolt-rig' principle.

The short section of 200lb mono is there purely to combat the tope's teeth. Even so, really big tope can, and will, chew through this during a longish fight. Some experienced anglers, therefore, still prefer to use 18 inches of 50lb wire crimped to the lower rolling swivel, which even big tope struggle to bite through – this or 300lb-plus mono.

Wired!

It's also interesting to note that in very shallow water tope will often pick up and drop bait fished on the heavy mono to the hook – whereas they rarely do this with the wire. You can often improve your catch rate if you change to a wire biting trace when the tope are continuously hitting and dropping the baits.

Coloured Up

Another good tip when using this rig is that when fishing over shallow rougher ground in

Build Sequence

01 Begin with a 60in length of 100lb mono.

02 To one end, tie on a size 2 rolling swivel.

03 Slide on a zip slider boom and a 5mm bead.

04 Now tie on another size 2 rolling swivel.

05 To the lower swivel, crimp on 20 inches of 200lb commercial-grade mono.

06 On the remaining free end of the 200lb mono, slide on a crimp and size 6/0 Mustad Viking 79515 hook. Crimp this in place to complete the rig.

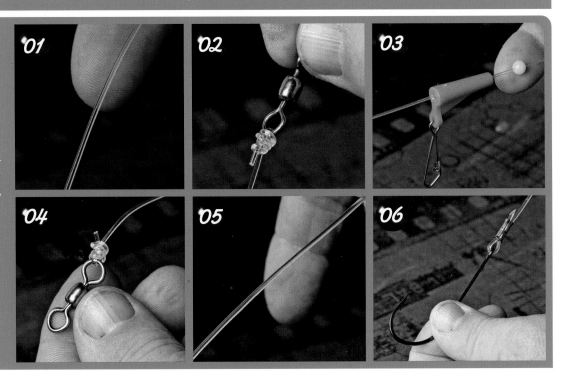

gin-clear water, the heavy mono stands out like a sore thumb. Try colouring the heavy mono with a black permanent marker and you'll see that the bite ratio to hook-ups improves dramatically. It also pays to use black-coloured swivels and crimps when fishing in very shallow, clear water because tope can be spooked by light glinting off a swivel that's adjacent to the bait. If you haven't fished for tope in gin-clear water of less than 10 feet deep, then you won't be aware of this.

Overkill!

It's also a fact that too many anglers still use ridiculously big hooks when tope fishing. A Mustad Viking 6/0 is easily big enough and strong enough to land the biggest tope swimming. There is no need for huge 8/0 and 10/0 hooks. These will cost you fish because tope generally like smaller baits – not whole fish – and hiding a 10/0 in a mackerel tail section with just the hook point showing is impossible. Also, the bigger hooks take too much pressure to sink in the hard mouth of a tope, especially if you're light-line fishing.

Abrasion

Even with the long trace length, experienced anglers still choose to use short, 15ft leaders of 60lb mono. This gives added insurance against abrasion should a tope run across snaggy ground, but also helps guard against body abrasion should a tope roll up in the line when being fought. If this happens it's usually a sign that the angler is playing the fish way too hard anyway.

If you want to cast this rig uptide, then simply hang the baited hook on the wires of the grip lead and cast. Air pressure will pull the hook off the wire during the initial stage of the cast to give perfect presentation on the sea bed.

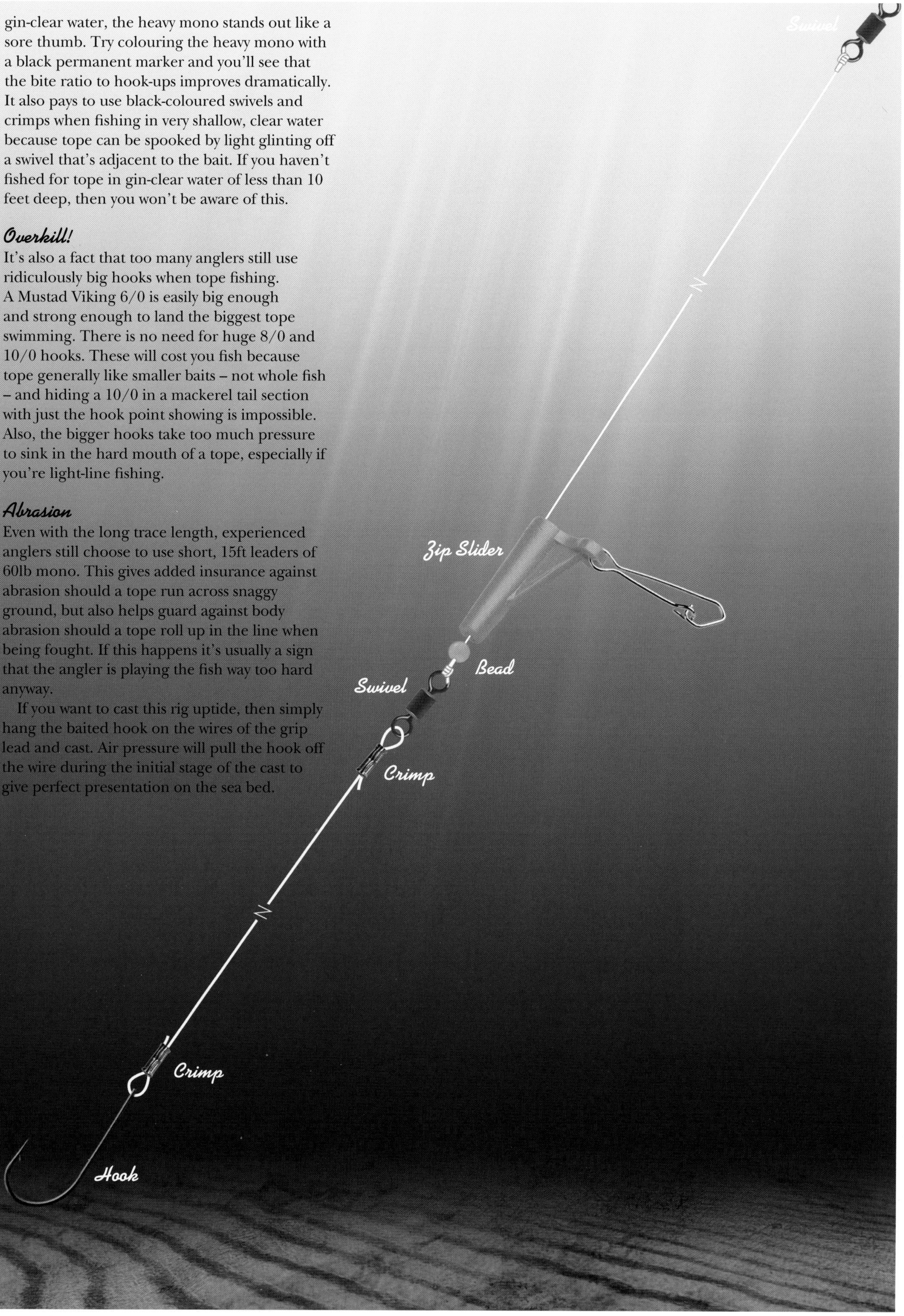

Swivel

Zip Slider

Bead

Swivel

Crimp

Crimp

Hook

EXTREMELY STRONG
EXTREMELY CASTABLE

HIDE OUT IN STEALTH BLUE CAMO

NEW STEALTH BLUE CAMO BRAID
FOR SALTWATER ADVENTURES

SPIDERWIRE

 NOTHING GETS AWAY™

SPIDERWIRE® STEALTH™

SPIDERWIRE-FISHING.CO.UK